THE CRACKER KITCHEN

A Cookbook in Celebration of
Cornbread-Fed, Down-Home Family
Stories and Cuisine

JANIS OWENS

SCRIBNER

New York London Toronto Sydney

SCRIBNER
A Division of Simon & Schuster, Inc.
1230 Avenue of the Americas
New York, NY 10020

First Scribner hardcover edition February 2009

SCRIBNER and design are registered trademarks of
The Gale Group, Inc., used under license
by Simon & Schuster, Inc., the publisher of this work.

For information about special discounts for bulk purchases,
please contact Simon & Schuster Special Sales:
1-800-456-6798 or business@simonandschuster.com

Designed by Kyoko Watanabe
Text set in New Century Schoolbook

Manufactured in the United States of America

1   3   5   7   9   10   8   6   4   2

Library of Congress Control Number: 2008032676

ISBN: 978-1-4767-4087-4

This book is for my father, foremost: Roy Junior Johnson, son of the South and Old Testament Prophet Extraordinaire. Also in honor of our great family cooks: Mama and Grannie and Big Mama; Aunt Doris and Aunt Izzy, Dessie and Grannie Hart; Jeana, Laurabell, and Burgerina—who taught me more lessons than I can remember, in the kitchen and every other room in the house. And finally, for Arkansas Wendel and my literary brothers, Pat Conroy and the late (and great and dearly grieved) Doug Marlette, whose unending delight in our shared Southern history informs this work.

Grace and peace to all of you, and to Daddy: Proverbs 20:7.

A truer verse, there never was.

What cracker is this same that deafs our ears with this abundance of superfluous breath?

—WILLIAM SHAKESPEARE,
KING JOHN, ACT II, SCENE 1, 1594

CONTENTS

INTRODUCTION

Pat Conroy

It was my great friend Doug Marlette who first brought me news of the amazing Florida novelist Janis Owens. He had met her at a book festival when he was publishing his first novel, *The Bridge,* and called to tell me he had found a new best friend for both of us. He was reading her first novel, *My Brother Michael,* and he didn't understand why Janis Owens wasn't famous. When I asked what was so great about her, Doug mentioned her pure authenticity, her comfortableness in her own skin, and her amazing gifts at storytelling. As Doug knew, I have a primordial attraction to the storytellers of the world. I ordered her three novels that night, and by the time I met Janis, I had read *My Brother Michael, Myra Sims,* and *The Schooling of Claybird Catts.* The three novels were an astonishment and a dilemma for me. She wrote about the hookwormed, xenophobic redneck South that has received such incessant ridicule in the literature of the South (including my own works) and in Hollywood movies that shiver with pleasure when their villains speak with those phony Southern accents. Janis used the term *Cracker* with affection and great understanding, and as I read her, I understood that she was awakening ghosts in my own kingdom that I would sooner or later have to interrogate if I was ever to understand the reign of both beauty and confusion in the life of my own mother, Peg Conroy. When

I finished reading the three books, I called Doug Marlette and echoed his question: "Why isn't Janis Owens world famous?"

When I read her cookbook, it was a revelation. She would refer to herself and her family as Crackers and Rednecks with pride and affection and a great tenderness. If I had ever called my family or my cousins rednecks, I think it doubtful that my mother would have talked to me again. Though my mother hailed from an Alabama family whose Cracker credentials were in perfect order, she spent much of her energy and all of her life in denial of this unassailable fact. She became a brilliant historian of her own life, and almost nothing she said about herself was true.

After my mother read *Gone With the Wind,* and after her total immersion in the character of Scarlett O'Hara, my mother reinvented herself. The young girl who had previously answered to the name of Frances changed her middle name to Margaret and ordered her family to call her Peggy, after her new heroine Margaret "Peggy" Mitchell. I learned this story on the day we buried my mother in the Beaufort National Cemetery. It was the same day my grieving stepfather, Dr. John Egan, said between sobs that it was "such an honor to be married to a Southern aristocrat." My mother was an open-field runner against her past. Because I adored everything about her, I think I let her turn me into the same thing.

Janis Owens's cookbook is a love letter written to celebrate the poor white people of the American South who were my mother's people and my own. Since Janis is incapable of writing a bad sentence, her cookbook is a joy to read and a pleasure to return to again and again. She has produced a Cracker Escoffier, or a White-Trash Julia Child, that is hilarious and charming. Her tour of Southern food seems definitive to me. She does not gussy up any of her recipes for stylistic or culinary reasons. It makes you hungry just to flip through the pages of this high-spirited and user-friendly book. It also took me to long-forgotten memories of my past.

I've often written about my mother's failure as a Southern cook. As a housewife in the fifties, my mother discovered the labor-saving pleasures of frozen food. Even today, I cannot pass a frozen chicken-pot pie without becoming bulimic. My brother Mike has a freezer full of them and eats them with relish whenever he feels nostalgic for Mom. Frozen macaroni and cheese is an abomination unto the Lord to me. When I escaped my mother's kitchen and entered The Citadel, I discovered that I had never eaten spinach, asparagus, Brussels sprouts, collard greens, and a whole produce department of other vegetables. Most cadets complained bitterly about the food in the mess hall, but I thought it was the finest food I had ever eaten, a cornucopia of guilty pleasures to discover and savor.

Yet, Janis's book caused me to remember some of the Southern dishes that my mother did well in the early years of her marriage. She could make perfect cornbread in a black skillet, and her fruit pies were legendary. Once a week, she composed a velvety lemon bisque that I could have inhaled with a straw. But it was in Piedmont, Alabama, and Orlando, Florida, that I feasted on the foods that Janis so lovingly describes in this cookbook. In Piedmont, my aunts and cousins would cook for hours preparing lunch for the men still in the fields. The meals were enormous, sensuous, and completely satisfying. Throughout the meal the women would burst out of the kitchen with some new steaming vegetable or fresh supply of biscuits. The gravies were heavenly, the fried chicken indescribable. Those were some of the happiest meals of my childhood.

In Orlando Aunt Helen and Uncle Russ would invite my family to the picnics at their Baptist church, and again, the recipes of Janis Owens were spread before my eyes in what seemed like endless profusion. When I asked my mother why Baptists ate so much better than Roman Catholics, she told me to shut up. I begged Aunt Helen to invite us to every church picnic that the Baptists organized, and if so, I promised not to fidget when she read from the Bible to my cousins, the Harper boys, each night. In Orlando I learned about congealed salads, aspics, deviled eggs, cole slaw, country ham, fried catfish, and dozens of other dishes that I had never encountered before. When we left Orlando, I thought that Baptists were the happiest, most well-fed people on earth. Later I'd tell my mother that I was thinking of becoming a Baptist so I would have lifetime access to those picnics, but Mother told me to hush up; if my father heard me, he'd kill me. I never brought up the subject again.

While reading several of the recipes in *Cracker Kitchen,* I burst out laughing because I'd never come across a recipe for roasted armadillo, rattlesnake, possum, or fried cooter. The world doesn't get any more Cracker than that, but I can't help but think that Janis is just showing out to make the outlander squeal. One of my favorite chapters is dedicated to Martin Luther King, Jr. It is her chapter on soul food and its intimate connection to Cracker cooking.

Janis Owens writes, *"Martin Luther King, Jr.'s birthday falls on January 15, and I offer up this soul-inspired menu in his honor and for all the rest of the heroes of the Movement: John Lewis and Ralph Abernathy and every single Yank, Jew, Episcopal pacifist, and student agitator among them. When they put their lives on the line and agitated Jim Crow into oblivion, they freed not only the people of color but also the children of the oppressor, who inherited the gift of diversity and eventually learned a better way (or at least some of them did; I did). It's a favor that can't be forgotten and won't be; not if this Cracker has anything to do with it."*

When I came to those words, their heartfelt generosity stunned me. What a large-souled woman Janis Owens is! I never thought I would read such a stirring declaration in a book celebrating the Cracker nation. I wrote a cookbook in 2004 that I modestly called *The Pat Conroy Cookbook*. In it you can find recipes for Duck Pappardelle with Black Truffle Sauce, Saltimbocca alla Romana, Soup de Poisson, and . . . well, you get my drift. Like my mother, I've been running away from the South my whole life, and I'll have to do a lot of walking backwards to get home again.

Janis Owens's cookbook is unpretentious, yet it sugarcoats nothing about the Cracker culture she celebrates and loves. The book is pitch perfect in tone and execution. She tells of a hidden, mysterious Florida that few people know about, and in so doing has written the best cookbook based in central Florida since Marjorie Kinnan Rawlings's *Cross Creek Cookery*. I wish my mother were alive so I could show her all the good times, and good food, that we missed.

WELCOME TO MY KITCHEN

L et me begin with a big country welcome to my kitchen. Just come on in and don't bother with the dog—he don't bite. Kick off your shoes and make yourself at home. Pour yourself some tea (there in the refrigerator; it should be cold) and brace yourself for a good feed, as Crackers aren't shy about eating but go for it full throttle, in it for the sheer, crunchy glory.

Though our roots are in the Colonial South, we are essentially just another American fusion culture, and our table and our stories are constantly expanding, nearly as fast as our waistlines. We aren't ashamed of either, and we're always delighted with the prospect of company: someone to feed and make laugh, to listen to our hundred-thousand stories of food and family and our long American past.

For Crackers are as indigenous to the New World as long-leafed tobacco, though we've never really been the toast of the town. We're the Other South: eighth-generation children of immigrants who came to America on big wooden ships long before the Civil War and steadily moved inland, the pioneers of three centuries. We mostly settled along the southern half of the eastern seaboard, long before the War of Secession, but we never darkened the doors of Tara or Twelve Oaks unless we were there to shoe mules or to work as overseers. We lived and thrived outside plantation society, in small towns and turpentine camps and malarial swamps. We're the Rednecks, the Peckerwoods, the Tarheels, and the Coon-ass, and a hundred other variations besides. We are the working-class back that colonial America was built upon, the children of its earliest pioneers, who have lately tired of hiding our light under a bushel, and have said to hell with all the subterfuge. We are who we are, and if you're curious what that exactly is, then pull up a chair, and I'll walk you through a bit of our history before we eat—or better yet, we can eat while we talk. Crackers have an inborn genius for both.

Before I begin, let me take a moment to validate my own Cracker pedigree and credentials, as I am what Princess Diana was to the English: a modern female scion of an ancient line born in rural Florida when Destin was a shallow, nameless bay and Orlando the shy younger sister of central Florida's true metropolis, Lakeland. I spent my youth moving here and yon in Louisiana and Mississippi, following Daddy's churches. (He was an Assembly of God preacher when I was born; later, a policy man with the Independent Life Insurance Company.) When I was nine, we returned to the heart of Cracker Florida, to Ocala. It was then a kitschy little tourist town where legendary herpetologist and showman Ross Allen ran what he called (without irony) a Reptile Institute out at Silver Springs.

Like most mid-century Crackers, we'd moved out of dog-trot houses by then and had traded up to a flat tract house in a treeless cookie-cutter subdivision, surrounded on all sides by recent Florida emigrants of every stripe. Rural Florida was still segregated back then, and from outward appearances we looked as assimilated as our white neighbors, except for the fact that we ate squirrel and talked like raccoons and carried pocket knives. We were something of a puzzle to everyone, even ourselves, as there were no accurate archetypes in contemporary American culture that reflected our particular past. Our great-great-grandfathers had fought and died for the Cause, and though we wept buckets at the railroad depot scene in *Gone With the Wind,* we had few emotional and historic ties to the ever-popular, ever-mythic Plantation South. There were no mincing Scarletts in our family line, but a lot of bonnet-clad, iron-willed matriarchs who dipped snuff, were fond of cane fishing, and on a lean day would go out, shotgun in hand, and shoot a flock of blackbird for supper.

We self-referred as Rednecks, Hillbillies, and Country Boys, shying away from the time-honored description: Crackers, as it was a name that had, in the latter half of the century, taken on a sinister connotation. Though the word had been in circulation for time out of mind, it had come to describe a portion of the population that was the nemesis of the social-gospel, julep-sipping South. Crackers were the Bad Guys in the Civil Rights Movement: crew-cut, toothless miscreants who wore George Wallace tie clips and used the N-word in combination with every adjective on earth. They were ill-read, over-churched, whiskey-addicted; prone to incest and hookworm.

We were some of that, and some not. (My Cracker grandfather's best friend was a black sharecropper, and a fellow black sawyer at the heading mill had once saved his life by lifting a truck off his chest.) Black people were intertwined in our history in a way that is hard to explain, and Old-school Crackers would willingly own up to mixed blood in a humorous manner ("a black cat in our alley"). But for the most part, having so much as a drop of black blood was taboo. Being white was our ace in the hole, you might say, and the single characteristic that set us apart from our fellow poor folk, though middle- and upper-class whites treated us with (if possible) more contempt than they did people of color.

We had no apparent excuse for our bad press and our bad teeth, and we returned their contempt in spades, with a whole encyclopedia of insults to describe upper- and middle-class whites: Big Shots, High-Hats, Collars, and the like. We preferred our own company to that of outsiders, and we maintained our ties with the land, even after our mass exodus into town, where we chased paychecks in sawmills and lumberyards, turpentine camps, and cattle runs in the early years of the century.

Our role as cultural outsider was so ingrained by then that we didn't overly labor to explain our histories to our fellow townies. We lived lives centered around our churches, marrying within them and giving much credence to the Lord's command to "come out from among them." We came out, and we stayed out. It wasn't till the late-nineteen seventies, when Disney moved to Florida and every Yankee on earth built a condo on the coast, that the lily-skinned Florida-born natives began to self-refer as Crackers as a way of separating their old Florida culture from the flood of Yankee transplants.

In this translation, being a Cracker meant your family had lived in Florida for at least three generations, had Southern roots, and among themselves, still talked like raccoons. It became a source of pride, and with Jimmy Carter's ascension to the presidency in the mid-nineteen seventies, the word gained national recognition as a way to describe white rural Southerners, though the root meaning was hotly debated and still frequently used as an insult, and no one really knew where it came from.

Well I, for one, found out, and here is the straight story on how we came to be named. It is not for the flat, salt-sprinkled bread baked by Nabisco, but from an ancient root word that dates back to Elizabethan England meaning "entertaining conversation" or "braggart" (the same root word for *crack,* as in crack a joke). It appears in Shakespeare and possibly the Bible (haven't nailed that one down yet, but Daddy's still looking), and like every other word in American English, it eventually evolved to a hardy noun, and an insulting one at that.

Long before the first cannon was fired on Fort Sumter, Cracker was slang for poor people; Corn Crackers so poor they only ate cheap corn instead of ground white flour. Slaves also used the term with contempt to describe the poor white overseers who cracked the whip on them in the fields. In pioneer Florida, the term was used to describe cow chasers or cowmen (never cowboys; they dislike the term) who hunted the remnants of the scrubby Spanish cattle in the sand and palmetto scrub. These lean, stringy cousins to the Texas longhorn weren't native to the state but had originally come to Florida in the mid-sixteen hundreds courtesy of the Spanish explorers. By the mid-eighteenth century they roamed free in the wilderness like wild deer and had to be driven from the palmetto scrub with whips that made a cracking sound; hence, *Cracker.*

By the turn of the century, the word had entered the American lexicon as a generic term for poor white people; though historically speaking, the original Crackers—corn eaters and cow hunters alike—were a generous mix of Scotch-Irish, Native Americans of all stripes, Spanish Conquistador, African slave, and even a pinch of the exotic—Moravian immigrant and Jewish trader. In pioneer central Florida, there were plenty of African American and Native American cowmen, though they were the exception. For the most part only white people were called Crackers, sometimes with affection, but mostly as an ethnic slur, roughly equivalent to the modern-day "trailer trash," or the like, connoting laziness or sorriness, or (by black people) ignorant bigotry.

The word and stereotype were so established by mid-century, that the figure of the ignorant Cracker made colorful entry into the literature of the day, a prime example being Bob Ewell, in the modern American classic *To Kill a Mockingbird.* If you have a copy on hand, flip to the scene about two-thirds of the way through, where Bob is on the witness stand at Tom's rape trial. His wisecracking, rooster-proud, racist demeanor is the personification of the Ignorant Cracker; as is Faulkner's Flem Snopes; Mr. Greenleaf in Flannery O'Connor's short story of the same title; and Ernest T. Bass on *The Andy Griffith Show.* (Ernest T is, of course, much more lovable; Mr. Griffith being a North Carolina Cracker himself. They call themselves *Tarheels* up there, and why, I do not know.)

If mid-century Crackers were upset by their less-than-sterling reputation in American letters, they kept it to themselves, as the running leitmotif of Cracker history is movement and survival and disdain for public opinion. They have always been a population in perpetual movement: They left Scotland for Ireland; then Ireland for the east coast of the New World; then inland into the Appalachians; and eventually down to the

Forever Frontiers of Indian Territory in the deep South. They fought yellow fever, mosquitoes, and a lot of insulted Native Americans on the way. Though they never really got on with the mosquitoes, they did marry a few hard-working Indians, and infused a good bit of Native American culture into their own Celtic stripe, along with every other ethnicity in Colonial America, which is just about every ethnicity you can name.

Thanks to their overweening fertility, they had as many children as they had hounds (which is to say: a *passel* of young'uns), and their best energies were given to basic survival: making a crop and feeding their families and bringing home a little cash for the store-bought items. Whenever they weren't scratching to make a dime, they gathered anywhere they could sit or squat (early Crackers were great squatters)—at country stores or crossroads or on the edge of a cut-over field—and while they whittled on a stick, they talked their heads off. For though they were famously taciturn around strangers, among themselves Crackers have always been—as Shakespeare surmised—big talkers, quick to gossip, to advise, or pass on a colorful family tale. I can personally vouch for the authenticity of the myth of the lovable old apron-clad Cracker Grannie, telling the young'uns stories on the porch.

If you doubt me, here is pictorial evidence: a shot taken in '62 when I was a toddler, sitting in my rocking chair in front of Grannie's house in Marianna. Her rocking chair, temporarily vacant, is behind me, casting a shadow on the far wall—a very long shadow, indeed. (Ah, metaphor! Where would Southern letters be without them?)

Look closely at the yard at my feet, and you'll see not a blade of grass. It's a swept yard, identical to old Bob Ewell's, though certainly the comparisons end there (Grannie was 100 percent Atticus Finch).

Storytelling (or telling "yarns" as it is sometimes called, though yarning has tall-tale implications and yarns are understood to be exaggerated) is a hallmark of Cracker life, as is our other chief source of entertainment: church. Whether it was the Scotch-Irish or the Native American influence, I really don't know, but I do know that Crackers have a fixation with religion, especially among the womenfolk, and an equally wide streak of superstition.

Since the Great Awakening, we've been mostly fundamentalist Christians; though historically speaking, Cracker Christianity is rigid with fear and shot through with the odd myth and a hundred little cautions and warnings. I figure this dark and brooding interpretation of Scripture sprang from the grind of pioneer lives lived on the cutting edge of death and wholly at the mercy of the elements. Corn is a water crop, and without irrigation a drought could wipe it out completely, as could a marauding deer (read *The Yearling*), a single hailstorm, or something as simple and commonplace as a late or early frost. There were no guarantees of longevity for the humans either.

Cracker life is built around a nearly pathological love of family, and in the days before penicillin and mosquito containment, a woman could lose a beloved baby to simple diarrhea, or a devoted husband to pneumonia, in a single day's time. My great-grandfather John Jackson went out a few days before Halloween in 1918 to gather his livestock in a storm, caught a cold that turned into pneumonia, and died two days later. His wife, my great-grandmother Emma, went on to remarry, and within the decade, her youngest son, Charlie-Boy, got a minor scrape in the field hoeing cotton and died of blood poisoning almost as quickly.

Every Cracker on earth can tell you of a dozen such tragedies, not from the distant past, but stark, unending domestic tragedy that happened in this century, within living memory. Our pioneer ancestors walked a fine line between heaven and earth and lived their lives accordingly, with much energy given to making right with the Lord, hoping that, with His divine favor, they could beat the odds and raise their children to maturity, or at least make a crop. Hence their love of the Eternal, and their particular affinity with Jesus, who loved His Mama and didn't take crap off the rich folk. They embraced Him with their entire hearts, and let me tell you, their love went deep (as does mine, now that I think of it). The women of Grannie's generation practically wallpapered their houses with Jesus pictures—of Him praying in the garden, knocking at the door, pondering Jerusalem. When my cousin Marcie and I went to clean out Aunt Izzy's house after Uncle Gene died, Marcie stood in the front door and asked incredulously, "What are we gonna do with all these *Jesus* pictures?" because standing in the front room alone, there were about eleven of them in plain sight.

I took a good many of them and have at least four hanging on my walls today. I personally think they're a little glimpse of Celtic superstition—the Cracker equivalent to Irish women's rosaries over the bed—but I never would have told Grannie that. (She would have suffered pangs of guilt over "worshiping graven images" and lost her joy in them and walked around like more of a crushed beetle than she already was.)

Many Crackers started out Baptist or shouting Methodist, but in the black belt and in heavily Native American areas, the Pentecostals gained ground in the early years of the century and the image of the barking-mad Cracker Holy Roller was born (of which I am a proud, card-carrying member). Their early church services were held in "brush arbors" and on the camp meeting circuit. Just between you and me (that means, don't tell Daddy), they drew much from Native American Green Corn tradition and African mysticism, overlaid on fundamentalist Christianity (and not a whit less valid for either).

Though these wild-eyed brush-arbor fanatics were the object of humor at the hands of Southern mainstream religion (we're talking Presbyterians here), Crackers themselves were tolerant of odd religious fancy. If an individual maintained what was called "clean living," he or she was respected whether Mormon, Pentecostal, Jewish, or Catholic. People were judged on their strictness of adherence, and if they fell short (Mormons drinking coffee, Jews eating bacon, Pentecostals sipping whiskey), they immediately lost their good reputations and cloaks of respectability. Where religion was concerned, extreme was good. Any talk of moderation was considered the rankest compromise, the lukewarm destined to be momentarily spewed out—a metaphor familiar in Cracker life, where everyone dipped or chewed. Spit cups were common, and things were constantly being *spewed* out.

In time, religion became the backbone of the Cracker social calendar. Beyond the twice- and, sometimes, three-times-a-week services, church life offered plenty of public interaction: ice-cream socials and dinner-on-the-grounds, and, of course, your steady round of funerals, which were attended in honor of the dead and for the opportunity to eat some really good cream corn. Most of the meetings were punctuated by food and laughter, as the thing with Cracker religion is that it is both sacred and self-deprecating. The best example I can think of is my old Pentecostal, fire-breathing Daddy, who runs a ham radio net called *Ambassadors for Christ*.

I tell a lot of Daddy stories when I speak, and I was being interviewed by Hank Connors on his radio show at the University of Florida, when he asked me on-air if Daddy was still a preacher.

"Oh, yeah," I assured him. "He's an Ambassador for Christ."

Hank started at my response, then hit the cough button and lowered his voice to ask, "*What* did you say?"

"Daddy," I repeated, "he's an Ambassador for Christ. That's the name of his show—his radio net."

Hank was visibly relieved. "I thought you said he was a *bastard* for Christ," he murmured, offering an opening no self-respecting Cracker could resist.

I grinned and assured him, "Oh, well, he's that, too."

We laughed so hard that the rest of the interview was just about inaudible, and when I got home, I hastened to call Daddy and repeat the conversation word for word. To his credit, Daddy laughed as long and hard as we had, without a blink of offense. The phrase "no laughing matter" is really not applicable to much in Cracker life.

And lest I paint the culture as overly sanctimonious (sanctimoniousness is poison to any self-respecting Cracker), let me point out that there was always, inevitably, a large and rowdy faction of unbelievers, anti-believers, and out-and-out doubters, who were casually referred to as backsliders, heathens, and sinners. Even the most respectable Cracker family had a few—easily identified by their cigarettes, tattoos, and preference for gathering at jooks and barrooms, where they drank more whiskey than iced tea (and from the same-sized tumblers). Their heathen tradition was even wilder than that of the Pentecostals (read Harry Crews), but like gopher turtles and rattlesnakes, the two cultures cohabited nicely, in no small part because the sinners were under no delusion about their fallen state and had every intention of getting saved two minutes before they died. (It only took two lines of prayer. How hard could it be?) In the meanwhile, they lived by a credo that could be best summarized by the inscription one of my brother's heathen friends wrote in his high-school yearbook: *Get drunk, raise hell, go naked.*

I think that pretty much sums it up.

Which is all to say that this particular subspecies of the very earliest Americans, which I will refer to as *Crackus Americanis,* was an unusually diverse and colorful band of humanity, which took root and flourished all over pioneer America in the latter century. And though their affiliation with whips, poor dental hygiene, and old-time religion gave them a really virulent case of bad PR, they eventually came to embrace their name with humorous deprecation, in no small part because they evolved into such an intractable and stubborn race that self-referring with a derogatory term suited them down to the ground.

Their whole persona was wrapped up in being independent, self-sufficient, and boldly against the grain. If you ever come across a multimillionaire central Florida cattle baron, chances are he'll be wearing worn jeans, ancient pointed-toed boots, and the straw cowboy hat he bought at Woolworth's for fifty cents in 1953. To dress otherwise would be "getting above his raising" or even worse, sleeping with the enemy (that is, pretending he's Presbyterian and eats only biscuits).

There is pride in that defiance and an inborn conviction that by adhering to the rules of fashion or buying into the myth that money buys happiness—well, that's the Cracker road to perdition. Soon you'll be putting sugar in your cornbread and drinking chai tea and sending your children to the Ivy League.

It's the thin end of the wedge.

My intention in writing this cookbook is to introduce readers (or for many, to reacquaint you) to this most original American subspecies that has greatly transcended its roots in the Colonial South, and now has children from Miami to Oregon, from Manhattan to California. This wide-ranging diaspora is well-documented along many tried and true migratory lines: Kentucky Crackers moved across the river to Ohio; Arkansans emptied out into Illinois, Arizona, and all points west; Alabamans packed up for Florida and Texas; and with the advent of the Greyhound bus, Georgia and Mississippi Crackers practically inherited the earth.

They left for the money, mostly, to labor in the coal mines of West Virginia and the engine shops of Detroit, and to become webfoot soldiers in service to our benevolent Uncle Sam. I've often wondered if there are any reliable statistics for how much of the military sprang from the Cracker South, for when I was a child, I never met a man who hadn't done at least a few stints in the army. These young Crackerlings roved about Europe and the Pacific theater and military bases all over the world, and when they returned home, a good many of them brought home foreign war brides. I'm not sure these young women—born in worn-torn cultures and worshipful of their American liberators—quite knew what they were getting into when they got involved with yarn-spinning Cracker men who wouldn't know the truth if it spit in their face.

Case in point is one of my husband's great-uncles, who fell in love with a comely German lass, whom he regaled with stories of his rich Southern heritage—all Tara and Twelve Oaks and polished marble floors. According to Grannie Hart, he took care to marry her "over there," and when he brought her home to meet the folks in northeast Arkansas, her shock was apparent to all.

"You should have seen her face when she come in the door," Grannie recalled with a shake of her head. "You could see her feathers fall."

I have an inkling many a naive war bride's feathers similarly fell, but no matter. The end result was another dab of fusion culture and an assimilation that has made Cracker DNA more diverse and widespread than one would first assume. We might seem a small, inbred minority, but over the years, we've entered the American mainstream with a vengeance and produced our share of cultural icons (Elvis comes to mind) and a few presidents (I won't name any names, but you know who you are) and a whole lot of KFC franchises, from sea to shining sea.

I personally think it's time we rise up and introduce ourselves beyond the closest crossroads, and I heartily welcome you into my kitchen to celebrate the three pillars of Cracker life: food and laughter and food.

Relax, unwind, and don't sweat the fine print. The only rule of Cracker cooking is there are no rules. Just come, enjoy, and make these recipes your own. Add pepper, delete pepper; toss in a stick of butter or make it rigidly fat free. The secret to our long survival is our innate Cracker ability to mutate to fit the circumstances. If you're married to a Chinese man and like soy sauce, then throw in some soy sauce. If you're a vegetarian, then substitute tofu. The only things really sacred in Cracker Culture are faith, the love of family, and a certain holy reverence for the gift of telling a story with perfect comedic timing. Everything else is negotiable, including our food, and if you doubt my sincerity, read ahead to my section on wild game feasts and roadkill.

We adapt, we hide. We emerge, we move to greener pastures. We marry outside the species, then convert them so thoroughly that soon they can't remember where they came from in the first place. We're like a kindly old virus, marching on, country to village to town, just like the bluebloods of Yoknapatawpha County feared. We are America's past, and along with every other diversity, we are its future.

Trust me on this one.

We're like cockroaches in that respect: We emerge, we forage, and we momentarily disappear, but not forever. If a nuclear holocaust ever takes place, the Crackers will be the first to crawl out of the rubble, looking for a pot so they can boil some grits to settle their nerves and offer a play-by-play of what they were doing the moment the bomb dropped. ("Was out standing in the yard, hanging out the wash, when *boom* it went. Shook the pecans *right* off the limbs.")

There will be a marked lack of real astonishment in the story, as Crackers have seen and done it all. We've won battles and lost them; raised children and adopted a few more. We got spunk, we got color, and there is nothing we love better than discussing our wonderfulness, so here we go.

I'm beginning with a most favored season in Crackerdom: Spring, with a few old favorites and modern twists, most of which have come into the culture via the infusion of modernity, primarily the birth of the citrus industry in central Florida, *Southern Living,* and *Gone With the Wind.* We were charmed by the former, and very nearly seduced into mass assimilation by the latter, wanting to move up to Tara and surrender our origins for a chance at life in the Big House. You know: trade our mules in for horses and marry one of the Tarleton twins and publicly renounce cornbread in favor of biscuits. (And when and, oh, when has that sort of cultural closeting ever paid off? Let me tell you something, ladies: Stuart Tarleton would be a fine husband in good sailing, but the first time you served him armadillo, he wouldn't touch it. He'd tell you to take your Cracker ass back to the kitchen and make him a *julep,* and you'd have no choice but to stab him with the same butcher knife you used to skin the armadillo, then bury him under the scuppernong arbor where you buried your first husband and had hoped to one day bury that *bitch* Scarlett, who was always mincing around, stealing other women's men.)

But enough of my yakking. Here's what you come for: Our occasionally nutritious and always delicious table, which is very nearly holy in Cracker Culture, a well-set table a sure sign of clean living and high moral fiber. It is one of the highest compliments any Cracker can get, male or female, rich or poor: they set a *fine* table. The other is: they come from *good* people. And the last: their children have done *well* for themselves. I like to think that I have admirably attained all three, or at least two of the three, on a good day.

You can, too. Here's how.

CHAPTER ONE

Crosses, Cakes, and Storytelling Over Coffins: It Must Be Spring

Spring in Cracker Nation is a colorful enterprise that comes on early. In mid-February the dormant dogwoods and redbuds quietly unfurl their blooms roughly two weeks before the mountains of fuchsia and white azaleas put on a much grander show. For real old-school Crackers, it is a season of calculated planting, seeds going in the ground according to the stages of the moon. With the help of the almanac, beans are planted on a certain day and watermelon yet another, and woe betide the man who gets anxious and plants too early, or lazy and plants too late.

Since I've never made a living farming, I judge the beginning of Spring with less stringent guidelines, and one simple gauge: the local hickory. When they come to bud and leaf, the frost is behind you and you're free to start your garden—the sooner the better, as the bugs will fight you for your tomatoes if you wait too long.

In my own childhood, Spring was a season of joyous freedom from heavy coats and piled blankets and, most joyous of all, shoes. I well remember that first day in early March when we'd go to Mama in committee, my brothers and I, and ask permission to take off our shoes for the summer. If it was too early or we'd been prone to colds, the answer was no. If it was warm enough and we were in sturdy good health, she'd answer yes. The first thing I'd do is run through the beds of green clover that covered our backyard: Ah! Ecstasy in bare feet! As far as I can remember, we never put them on again, except for church and school, till first frost in early October. We were barefoot and proud of it, and even today I possess the unique Cracker ability to walk across a broiling Florida parking lot in bare feet without a skip or a flinch, with the equanimity of a Hindu fire walker.

Foodwise, Spring is a remarkably social season with many gatherings—graduations, wedding showers, and, of course, the ever-popular funeral feed, that isn't so much a celebration of death as much as a defiance of it. When you eat some of my chicken perloo or real creamed corn, you will say, with St. Paul of old, "O death, where is thy sting?"

But first there are Easter Eggs. There are pastel hats and white gloves and children's processionals with palm fronds and agonizingly memorized bits of Scripture. There is, in short, Easter.

I. EASTER

MENU

Crab Bisque

Easter Ham

Potatoes au Gratin

Green Bean Bundles

Mama's Cornbread

Cracklin' Cornbread

Easter Bunny Cake

Iced Tea *(page 252)*

Light Lemony Iced Tea *(page 254)*

I understand that Roman Catholics call the week before Easter Passion Week or Passiontide, but in mostly Protestant Cracker Nation, Easter is identified more with last-minute trips to K-Mart for matching hosiery than Maundy Thursday retreats to convents and the washing of feet.

We seem to have lost something in translation, and considering the fact that Easter is a holiday built around the remembrance of a painful public execution (the Crucifixion), it really has evolved into a lighthearted festivity. It offers the opportunity to go all out and really dress up, old and young alike, presenting a photo-op that no respectable Cracker can stand to pass up. On the next page is a classic Easter shot of me and Grannie, posed on our porch in Metairie when I was three.

Grannie always wore a hat and gloves to church (and to town, too, for that matter), but I was, even then, a less sophisticated breed of Cracker. It was only when the little Catholic girl next door came home early from Mass and offered her Easter hat

for a quick photo that I agreed to be captured on film in full Easter regalia, patent-leather Mary Janes crossed at the heels, looking pretty pleased with my three-year-old self.

Since Sunday morning church (or Mass) is part and parcel of the holiday, the day's menu usually stars some old-school favorites that can be cooked slowly in an oven, or better yet, cooked ahead of time and warmed up after the Easter pictures are taken.

Crab Bisque

To begin, I offer a soup that is common along the coast of Cracker Florida and versatile enough to be used as the starting course of any menu in this book: the ever-delicious Crab Bisque. Since I live near a working fishing village (and a lovely one at that: Cedar Key), I have good access to fresh crab, which makes this modest little cream soup truly spectacular. It's a little on the rich side, and a small bowl will do if it's a meal starter.

1 tablespoon sweet butter
1 tablespoon plain flour
¾ teaspoon ground sea salt
⅛ teaspoon ground black pepper
½ small Vidalia onion, finely chopped
2 cups whole milk
½ cup light cream
Pinch of paprika
6 ounces fresh crabmeat, cleaned and picked out
1 tablespoon cooking sherry
1 tablespoon finely chopped chives

1. Put the butter, flour, salt, pepper, onion, milk, and cream in a blender and whirl till smooth.

2. Add the paprika and crab and pulse a few times till well blended.

3. Pour the mixture into a medium-sized, heavy-bottomed saucepan and heat to a simmer over medium-low heat. Let simmer for 2 to 3 minutes, till warm and slightly thickened, stirring to make sure it doesn't scorch.

4. Stir in the sherry and sprinkle the chopped chives on top.

Makes 4 cups

Easter Ham

Some people swear by their Easter roasts, but Mama always made ham for Easter—a big one, cooked in sugar and usually cool by the time we got around to eating it. This version is both delicious and doggone convenient, as it is precooked and all you're really doing is sweetening it up with its little soda soak, then baking that sugar in. The resulting ham has all the hallmarks of a Classic Cracker favorite: easy and delicious and it makes your house smell good while it's baking.

You can't ask more of a ham than that.

One 12-ounce can cola
⅓ cup packed light brown sugar
One cooked 5-pound ham

1. In a large sealable bag, mix the cola and sugar till dissolved. Add the ham and shake it around to make sure it's coated.

2. Marinate overnight in the refrigerator, occasionally giving it a shake to make sure the marinade stays on the ham.

3. Preheat the oven to 350°.

4. Put the ham in a roasting pan and bake for 1 hour, basting once or twice. Let it cool a few minutes before slicing. Serve right away, or later, cold.

Serves about 8 regular people, or 4 Crackers,
depending on how long the Easter service went

Potatoes au Gratin

There are many marriages of flavor in Cracker cooking so popular they are repeat performers at every table. Ham and potatoes and cheese are three of them; a ménage à trois that combines the smoothness of white potatoes, the sharp zest of Cheddar cheese, and the sweet saltiness of sugared ham. There isn't a taste bud in your head that won't dance when you take a bite of this trio.

4 cups peeled and thinly sliced white potatoes
½ cup salted butter
3 tablespoons plain flour
1 cup sour cream
½ cup whole milk
1½ cups shredded sharp Cheddar cheese, divided
½ teaspoon salt
½ teaspoon ground black pepper
Dash of hot sauce

1. Preheat the oven to 325°.

2. Fill a large pot with water and put your potatoes in. Bring it to a boil and boil 2 to 3 minutes.

3. Drain the potatoes. Spray a 9 x 13-inch baking dish with nonstick cooking spray and spread the potatoes in it in a thin layer.

4. Melt the butter in a medium saucepan over medium heat. Sprinkle in the flour and stir till blended.

5. Stir in the sour cream, milk, 1 cup of the cheese, the salt, pepper, and hot sauce. Cook, stirring, over medium-low heat till smooth, adding more milk to thin it if necessary.

6. Pour the cream mixture over the potatoes. Bake for 30 minutes, till bubbling.

7. When you take the potatoes out of the oven, top it with the remaining ½ cup cheese and let it sit for 5 minutes, till melted.

Serves 6

Green Bean Bundles

This treasure of green beanery comes from the kitchen of my best friend, Carole, who goes by the pet name Burger (or Burg, or Burgette, or Burgerina; the variations are endless; her husband calls her Sweet Cat).

Anyway, Old Burg is the poster child of modern Cracker womanhood: sinewy, hard working, hard cooking, and (apparently) blonde till death do us part. Nowadays we're both getting more than a little gray and her eternal blondeness poses less of a threat, but years ago, when we were young Cracker wives, she truly feared that she'd die in some unforeseen and inopportune moment between dye jobs and would be laid out in a coffin with dark roots showing. She had me and her other BFF, Shari, promise we'd come to the funeral home if such a thing happened and touch up her roots before the funeral; she really did.

I never told either of them but can now confess that I really dreaded the idea of an evening spent with Burger's corpse and Lady Clairol. Fortunately for all of us, nothing of the sort ever happened. We've survived to middle age, hale and hardy as ever, and old Burg might have gone to her grave with her reputation as a natural blonde intact, if not for, well, the story I just told.

What are best friends for?

One bite of her Green Bean Bundles and you will agree that these green beans (and any other recipes hereafter attributed to her) are supreme-o.

**4 cups whole young green beans, snapped into
3-inch lengths and stringed (frozen will do
if fresh isn't available)**
Six 6-inch long bacon strips, halved crosswise
6 tablespoons salted butter
½ cup packed brown sugar
1 tablespoon minced fresh garlic
1 tablespoon cold water
½ teaspoon salt
½ teaspoon freshly ground black pepper

1. Preheat the oven to 375°.

2. Gather 12 to 15 of the beans and tie them together with a strip of the halved bacon. Insert a toothpick to keep the bundle together. Repeat with the remaining beans and bacon.

3. Place the bundles close together in a 9 x 13-inch baking pan.

4. Melt the butter in a medium saucepan over low heat and mix with the sugar, garlic, water, salt, and pepper. Pour over the bean bundles.

5. Cover the pan with aluminum foil and bake for 45 minutes. Uncover and bake for 20 minutes more.

Serves 4 to 6 and can be doubled

Mama's Cornbread and Cracklin' Cornbread

Now cornbread is as good an example of Cracker ingenuity as I can think of. Corn really isn't European at all but was introduced by our equally ingenious Native Americans, who raised the lowly grain to sacred status, calling it *maize*. Our earliest species of *Crackus Americanis* borrowed the recipe (or more likely, took an Indian wife) and were soon embracing it with equal reverence, though it had a few unintended consequences. Anthropologists claim that the Confederates lost the War Between the States because of its citizens' overconsumption of poorly ground corn, which wreaked havoc with their digestive tracts. They theorize that dysentery killed almost as many Rebels as did the Yanks. (Corn, of course, disputes the claim.)

An even more insidious consequence of our all-encompassing love of corn was the scourge of pellagra that rose to epidemic proportions in the early years of the century and claimed the lives of my great-great-grandfather and at least three of his children, who died most ignoble deaths behind the wire at Milledgeville (for the uninitiated, one of three mental institutes in the deep South, along with Tuscaloosa and Chattahoochee). The root cause of their insanity was a mystery at the time but later traced to a niacin deficiency thanks to their Crackeresque overdependence on corn.

Here's a picture of the old boy in a better day: Hortensious Rudd. His brothers were Cicero and Demosthenes. He survived four years as a webfoot private in the Calhoun Grays (CSA) and a couple of cold winters as a POW at Camp Chase, Ohio, only to give his life (or at least his sanity) to corn.

But, hey, why drag up a few unfortunate incidents of corn passion, when so many good examples of healthy and moderate consumption abound? The recipe for cornbread I offer here belongs to my mother and is truly a Mythic use of Maize. She cooks it (always, no exception) in a hot black iron skillet and on special occasions throws in a cup of cracklin's—that is, fried pig fat. Then, my friend, you have a feast, no matter what else is on the table. I am convinced my husband married me because of my mother's cornbread, which she makes especially for him because he brags on it so much. He says no one else's cornbread, including mine, compares.

Mama's Cornbread

1½ cups plain yellow cornmeal
1½ cups self-rising flour
1 teaspoon baking powder
½ teaspoon baking soda
Pinch of salt
2 large eggs, beaten
1½ cups buttermilk
6 tablespoons bacon drippings or
       melted butter, divided

1. Preheat the oven to 375°.

2. Combine the dry ingredients in a large mixing bowl, and blend well.

3. Add the eggs, buttermilk, and 3 tablespoons of the bacon drippings and stir till smooth.

4. Heat the remaining 3 tablespoons bacon drippings in a 9-inch cast-iron skillet over medium-high heat for 1 minute till hot but not smoking. Shake the pan to coat the bottom.

5. Pour the cornbread batter into the hot skillet. Bake for 20 minutes, till brown on top and crispy brown on the bottom.

Serves 5

Cracklin' Cornbread

Cracklin' Cornbread is a Cracker favorite and a simple variation on my mother's recipe. You'll find your cracklin's—fried pork skin—in the meat section at the grocery store. Buy a bag and bring them home, then soak a cup of them in water for a half hour to soften. Drain and make your cornbread according to the preceding recipe, adding the cracklin's in step 3, when you add the buttermilk. Cook just the same, and when it is done, use a sharp serrated knife to cut into wedge-shaped portions.

Eat hot with ham dishes or a vegetable plate, or cold with a glass of buttermilk. It will restore your faith in mankind. It will make you understand why some of my people went nuts over their passion for corn. It will make you proud to be associated with such an upstanding grain.

Easter Bunny Cake

I have been making this goofy cake since I was a teenager, and it is still a big hit for the Easter crowd. I make him a chocolate brown bunny because one of my daughters doesn't like coconut, but he is particularly fuzzy and attractive when you make him with vanilla frosting sprinkled with coconut. As always, freshly grated coconut is best, but canned or bagged coconut will do if you're pressed for time or really detest grating.

CAKE

> **1 box white cake mix, baked in**
> **two layers according to**
> **package directions**

ICING

> **6 tablespoons sweet butter,**
> **softened**
> **½ cup unsweetened cocoa powder**
> **2½ cups powdered sugar**
> **¼ cup whole milk**
> **1 teaspoon vanilla extract**
> **(real extract is best)**

Jellybeans and red licorice
½ cup fresh grated coconut

1. Bake the cake mix and let cool.

2. To make the frosting, beat together the butter, cocoa, and sugar. Gradually beat in the milk and continue to beat until you have a light butter cream frosting. Beat in the vanilla.

3. To assemble the bunny, put one cake layer on a foil-covered cookie sheet. This is your bunny head. Ice it with chocolate frosting. Cut out a bow-tie shape from the remaining layer and fit it under the bunny's head, then cut out a couple of bunny ears and put them on top of the bunny's head.

4. Frost the bow tie and ears. (Make vanilla icing for a white bunny; because of the cocoa, mine is a brown bunny.) Put on jellybean eyes and a smiling red licorice mouth. Sprinkle the bow tie with coconut or chocolate chips or whatever festive decoration appeals to your creative eye.

Serves 6

II. BRIDAL AND BABY SHOWERS

MENU

Cold Chicken Salad with Pecans and Tarragon

Texas Sweet Onion Pie

Sister Jackson's Sausage Cheese Balls

Easy Dill Dip

Cold Coconut Cake

Abby's Pound Cake

Cream Cheese Vanilla Icing

Candied Pecans

Pineapple-Banana Punch

Late in spring, just about the time that final exams and high school graduations loom, a great rash of showers appears on the horizon. Not spring rain, but baby and wedding showers, along with teas, book club meetings, and all manner of polite crystal-and-cloth-napkin affairs. There seems to be a certain competition among hostesses over how much food is served at these affairs. I have been to bridal showers where the spread of dishes never ends, but trails off into the distance in all its sparkling crystal and silver splendor, on and on, enough food to feed Pharaoh's Army (as my mother would say).

Here are a few tried-and-true suggestions for your own lady lunches or showers. They are light and cold and guaranteed to impress. Furthermore, they are homemade. When your competition—you know, the coworker or snooty neighbor who is always criticizing your children—arrives with a bakery cake in a box, you can narrow your eyes, flatten your ears, and purr, "Oh, a *store*bought cake. How niiiiice."

Cold Chicken Salad with Pecans and Tarragon

There are hundreds of variations on chicken salad and, again, there are no rules. I'm using chopped pecans and tarragon in this one, but you can substitute chopped almonds or walnuts and make it fruitier by adding green grapes or diced apples. I prefer this one with tarragon, which isn't a common herb in Crackerworld but is gaining ground thanks to its mildly sweet flavor, kindly collaboration with chicken, and the fact it has a name that is multisyllabic, but phonetically simple to pronounce. It has no equivocal "th" sound, like that miserable Thyme (pronounced *Time? Tha-yme?*), which if mispronounced can lead to lifted eyebrows (annoying) or public corrections (embarrassing). It is an herb you can name-drop without fear of contradiction.

4 boneless, skinless chicken breast halves
½ cup diced celery
½ cup chopped pecans
½ cup mayonnaise
½ cup sour cream
Dash of soy sauce
1 teaspoon chopped fresh tarragon
Salt and freshly ground black pepper to taste

1. Fill a medium pot with water and bring it to a boil. Add the chicken and boil for 10 minutes. Pour off the water, cool the chicken, and shred it.

2. In a large mixing bowl, mix the chicken, celery, pecans, mayonnaise, sour cream, soy sauce, and tarragon. Season with salt and pepper. Chill for at least 1 hour before serving.

Serves 6

Texas
Sweet Onion Pie

My oldest daughter, Emily, married into a clan of straight-up obnoxious Texans, who take every opportunity to crow over their innate Texas ability to do everything bigger, better, and spicier than the rest of us washed-out old Florida Crackers. I usually grant their megalomania no quarter, but on the matter of Sweet Onion Pie, I have to bow to perfection and admit: Well, dang. Maybe they got something there.

I don't know why this pie is so astounding, but it is. A mild and memorable marriage of those old Cracker favorites—sweet onions and bacon and sour cream—it can be made ahead and warmed before serving. It is great for showers and brunches; actually it's pretty great anytime.

One 9-inch Flaky Pie Crust (page 258)
5 strips thick-sliced apple-cured bacon
3 tablespoons sweet butter
3 cups sliced sweet onions (Georgia Vidalia
　　　　gets my vote, but there are many Texas
　　　　sweet onions if you're a stickler)
2 cups sour cream
3 tablespoons plain flour
2 large eggs, beaten
¾ teaspoon salt
1 teaspoon coarsely ground black pepper

1. Preheat the oven to 325°.

2. Bake the pie crust for 10 minutes, then set it aside while you make your filling.

3. Fry the bacon in a cast-iron skillet till just crisp. Cut it into ½-inch pieces and return it to the skillet.

4. Add the butter to the bacon and let it melt. Add the onions and sauté over medium heat for 5 minutes, till lightly browned.

5. Pour the onion mixture into the partially baked pie crust.

6. Blend together the sour cream, flour, eggs, salt, and pepper in a mixing bowl and pour the mixture over the onions and bacon.

7. Bake for 30 minutes, until firm. Let cool to set a bit before serving.

Serves 6

Sister Jackson's
Sausage Cheese Balls

When I was pregnant with my first daughter and poor as a mouse, my mother's best friend, Sister Betty Jackson, threw me the shower to end all showers and prepared a spread as yet unmatched in baby-shower history. Here are her signature Sausage Cheese Balls, along with my own easy dill dip. Serve hot if you can, and if you can't, eat them anyway, as they're mighty good cold.

1 pound bulk sausage
4 cups shredded sharp Cheddar cheese
2½ cups baking mix, such as Bisquick
1 tablespoon dried minced onion
1 tablespoon horseradish sauce

1. Preheat the oven to 375°.

2. Put all the ingredients in a large bowl and squash together with your hands, as if you're kneading bread, till well mixed.

3. Shape the dough into walnut-sized balls and arrange 1 inch apart on a lightly greased baking sheet.

4. Bake for 20 minutes, till brown and sizzling. Serve with the dill dip.

Makes 5 to 6 dozen

Easy Dill Dip

This light spring dip goes well with vegetable trays and ordinary potato chips (potatoes + dill is another happy marriage of flavor). Your best crystal dip bowl will be honored to display it.

1 cup mayonnaise
1 cup sour cream
1 tablespoon finely chopped dill—fresh is
    best but dried will do
½ teaspoon ground sea salt
½ teaspoon freshly ground black pepper

Mix all the ingredients in a medium bowl. Cover and let stand for at least 30 minutes to allow the flavors to blend. Garnish with a pretty sprig of dill if you're going for Blockbuster Presentation.

Makes 2 cups

Cold Coconut Cake

Of all the cakes I make, this is my father's favorite; a modern, post-refrigeration creation that combines all the old Cracker favorites, including fresh coconut. Since it partially springs from a boxed mix and doesn't have boiled frosting, it is a snap to make and even the Laziest Cracker can adopt it as his or her own signature cake. The end result is almost like ice-cream cake but lighter.

Eat and be glad, or even better, serve at a shower and make the bakery cakes look like cardboard.

1 box white or coconut cake mix
2 tablespoons vanilla extract, divided
One 16-ounce tub whipped topping, thawed
One 16-ounce carton sour cream
1 cup powdered sugar
1 pound freshly shredded coconut, divided

1. Mix the cake mix ingredients, adding 1 tablespoon of the vanilla, according to the package directions. Bake in three thin layers in 9-inch cake pans till just golden. Pop the cakes out of the pans and let cool completely.

2. Blend the whipped topping, sour cream, and powdered sugar in a large mixing bowl, then beat till smooth.

3. Add the remaining 1 tablespoon vanilla and two-thirds of the shredded coconut and beat until blended.

4. When the cake layers are completely cool, frost with the cream mixture, then top with the remaining coconut.

5. Put the cake in an airtight container and refrigerate for at least 2 hours or, even better, overnight.

Serves 6

Abby's Pound Cake

Abby is my middle daughter, and though she has never been much more than rail thin, she has eaten a bowl of ice cream every day of her life, and pound cake whenever she can talk me into baking one for her. Here is her favorite recipe, which isn't the old-school Cracker lemon pound cake but Mama's cream-cheese recipe, that is two parts butter and one part cream cheese. You can vary this by adding lemon flavoring, or orange, or chocolate chips, or all of the above. I don't ice it with anything, since God knows it's fat enough as it is, but if you can stand the guilt, feel free.

> 1½ cups sweet butter, softened
>   (never margarine, heaven forbid)
> One 8-ounce package cream cheese,
>   softened
> 3 cups sugar
> 2 cups self-rising flour
> 1 cup plain flour
> Pinch of baking soda
> 6 large eggs
> 2 teaspoons vanilla extract
> 2 teaspoons brandy flavoring

1. Preheat the oven to 325°.

2. Beat together the butter and cream cheese in a mixing bowl. Add the sugar and blend well.

3. Mix the self-rising and plain flours and baking soda in a separate bowl. Add 1 cup of the flour mixture to the butter mixture and beat till blended. Add 2 of the eggs and beat till blended. Repeat, alternating eggs and flour. Don't overmix or the texture will be grainy. Mix till it looks fairly smooth without any big lumps.

4. Stir in the vanilla and brandy. Pour the batter into a 12-cup tube cake pan that has been sprayed with nonstick cooking spray.

5. Bake for about 1 hour. If you're not sure it's done, carefully open the oven door and stick a toothpick into the cake. If it comes out clean, you're done. If it is covered in uncooked goo, then bake for another 15 minutes, then check it again. I like mine medium brown, since the crust is the best part of all.

6. When it is done, sit it on the stovetop to cool. Run a knife carefully around the edge and pop it onto a serving plate and serve warm.

Serves 6 to 8

Cream Cheese Vanilla Icing

This is a tried-and-true version of light cream cheese icing—almost a glaze—just in case you didn't get enough fat in the cake.

2 cups powdered sugar
3 ounces cream cheese, softened
¼ cup sweet butter, softened
1 teaspoon vanilla extract
1 to 2 tablespoons whole milk

1. Mix the sugar, cream cheese, butter, vanilla, and 1 tablespoon milk in a mixer bowl till well blended, then beat for a minute or so to make it fluffy. If the icing is too thick to spread, thin it with milk, 1 teaspoon at a time.

2. When the icing is the desired thickness, spread it on top of the warm pound cake and let it dribble down the sides.

3. Let your favorite child lick the bowl, or if there is no current favorite, lick it yourself.

Serves 6

Candied Pecans

One of my buddies in the Newberry Garden Club gave me this recipe years ago after a Christmas party where I dined almost exclusively on candied pecans. You can use them to top ice cream or eat them out of a bowl, like peanuts. If you're looking for variation, add ½ teaspoon cinnamon at the end, when you're tossing the pecans in the syrup. Store in an airtight container and refrigerate to prolong life. Like most nuts, they freeze well.

4 cups pecan halves
1 cup firmly packed brown sugar
½ cup water
½ teaspoon vanilla extract

1. Preheat the oven to 350°.

2. To toast the pecans, spread them on a cookie sheet and bake for 5 minutes, till the kitchen smells like roasted pecans. Clean and butter the cookie sheet.

3. Put the brown sugar and water in a medium saucepan and heat over medium-high heat to the soft-ball stage (see Note).

4. Take the sugar syrup off the heat and stir in the pecan halves and vanilla, coating the pecans well. Turn the pecans out on a buttered cookie sheet and let cool for at least 1 hour. When they're cooled, crack them up and serve.

Makes 6 cups

Note: To tell if the syrup is at the soft-ball stage, fill a coffee mug halfway with cool water. Drop a drip of the cooking sugar syrup in the water. If it dissolves, keep the syrup bubbling on the heat and try again in a minute. When the drip hits the cool water and maintains a soft shape, you're in business.

Pineapple-Banana Punch

I married in a First Assembly of God Church in Ocala, Florida, and the walls of the fellowship hall would have fallen in like the walls of Jericho if so much as a thimble of liquor had been served. Here is the punch we drank, with a nice Florida Cracker citrus bite. I tell you what: after twenty-eight years, it is still my favorite fruit punch. It is sweet, fruity, and altogether good. Presbyterians can add champagne if they must, which would make it Pineapple-Banana Presbyterian Punch.

1 cup sugar
3 cups water
One 46-ounce can unsweetened pineapple juice
One 6-ounce can frozen condensed orange juice
3 large ripe bananas, mashed
2 liters ginger ale, chilled
Maraschino cherries for garnish

1. The day before (or month before, or week before) cook the sugar and water in a large saucepan over medium heat for 3 minutes, till the sugar is dissolved.

2. Stir in the pineapple and orange juices and bananas. Pour into plastic storage containers and freeze solid.

3. To make the punch, thaw the frozen fruit mixture for at least 1 hour, till it is at a hard slushy stage.

4. Mix half the slush with 1 liter chilled ginger ale right in the punch bowl and replenish with both as needed. For color, garnish with maraschino cherries.

Serves 12 to 15

III. FUNERAL FARE

Roast Chicken

Chicken Gravy

Chicken Perloo

Chinatown Chicken Almond

White Beans and Ham

Sweet Potato Pie

Sweet Potato Cream Pie

⬤

Parting is all we know of heaven,
And all we need of hell.
—EMILY DICKINSON

⬤

Listing funeral food right after a bridal shower may seem either pointedly ironic or a little ghoulish, but in Cracker Nation, we look on funerals as moments of both piercing grief and equally piercing joy; truly all we know of heaven, and all we need of hell. Hell is the very permanence of death, especially if the departed is a child or a spouse. Heaven is our belief that our dearly departed go there directly—do not pass go or inherit two-hundred dollars. Or at least Mama and I believe that way. Daddy, in his infinite hairsplitting wisdom, doesn't believe in the old absent-in-the-body-present-in-the-spirit notion and takes great offense when it's preached at funerals (which it always is around here, almost without fail).

As far as I can understand, he thinks we go to heaven sans body and flit around like little Casper-the-Friendly-Ghosts till the Judgment Seat of Christ. He has explained it many times to me, but I don't think I've quite grasped the nuance of the belief. Once, coming home from a funeral in South Alabama, he expanded this particular article of doctrine for the length of the long drive through the flat woods of Taylor County. Mama was asleep in the backseat for most of the lecture but woke up for the last twenty minutes and sat there, blinking and sleepy, till Daddy finally ran out of steam.

She let a pause gather in the quiet car for a long moment, then added her two cents in a small, modest voice, "Well, I just don't want to go to hell, is all."

I wholeheartedly agree and think that may be the heart of all Cracker religion: When all is said and done, we just don't want to go to hell, is all.

But enough of this talk of doctrine. We were speaking of funerals, and here is a shot of granddaddy taken at his brother John's funeral, in North Georgia, circa 1942.

According to family legend, Uncle John was the constable of Aetna County and spent most of the thirties breaking up everyone's still but his own. He was Granddaddy's favorite brother, and though Granddaddy and Grannie were poor as church mice when he died, Granddaddy somehow got up enough money to take the trip to Georgia for the burial. He made sure his attendance was remembered by standing up behind the crowd. See him? Right behind the preacher? That's my grandfather, James Isaac Rice, brother of John Rice. Good men, both. May they rest in peace.

The lighter side of the Cracker funeral comes when the dearly departed is safely interred, when the mourners retire to a relative's house or the fellowship hall of the church to eat, chat, and maybe take the stage and tell a few hilarious stories on the recently departed.

"Telling stories on them" it is commonly called, and the funnier the story, the better.

My uncle Kelly was the Prince of the hilarious family story, and at any family gathering, funeral or otherwise, would get going on someone, usually Grannie or her sister, my aunt Izzy, who would laugh as hard as the rest of us when he took the stage and got on a roll. Aunt Izzy was once almost killed in a freak car accident, and when she recovered, she eventually got a ten-thousand-dollar settlement for her pains; at the time considered a princely sum.

Through the years, Uncle Kelly worked it into a hilarious little tale, with Aunt Izzy (who was old-school Pentecostal, she didn't even cut her hair) as the seemingly innocent, but sly, litigant, who barely makes her bent way down the aisle of the court-room, till she gets the check in hand, when she tosses aside her cane with a big, "Thank ye, Judge!" and skips away.

"Oh, she made a mint that day," he'd intone, his Irish blue eyes snapping, "left that courtroom a rich woman—a *thousand-aire*," to roars of laughter on every side.

The source of all funeral hilarity is that old stiff-necked Cracker defiance, that insistence on keeping your head high and your pride intact no matter what foul ball life throws your way. Give us a life-threatening car wreck, and we spin it into a hilarious story. Give us death and we laugh even louder. In my experience, Crackers are as beset with melancholy as their distant kinsmen across the sea, the Celts and Irish, and like them, answer death and loss with laughter and more laughter. We don't go quietly into that dark night, nor do we go thinly.

We go feasting, cracking jokes, and giving death the back of our hand, and technically speaking, just about any recipe in this book can be brought to a funeral—beef, pork, or fowl; savory or sweet; as long as it is a good traveler (that is, can be easily packed and can be eaten cold). If your dearly departed attended church for any length of time at all, you can be assured that there will be so much food that no one will worry when your particular roasted chicken runs out, because there is plenty more where that came from.

The exception would be the wild beast section. I could see how if you brought along a possum to an after-funeral feast, the family of the deceased might take it as a thinly veiled insult. I'd stick to chicken if I were you, and if you have a really funny story about the departed, fight your way to the front and take the floor and tell it while everyone is eating. You'll feel better and everyone else will, too.

Roast Chicken

If there is one recipe in this book anyone can master, it is roast chicken, which is simplicity itself and not half as labor-intensive as frying. It could be argued that it's healthier, but since I baste with the drippings and a little butter and garlic and top it off with gravy, that's debatable. It's a good traveler for funerals or for dinner-on-the-grounds or what have you. It's also good at home, with smashed potatoes or brown rice.

> **1 chicken or hen, about 4 pounds**
> **¼ cup salted butter**
> **2 tablespoons dried minced onion**
> **2 cloves garlic, crushed through a press**
> **Seasoning salt and ground black pepper**
> **   to taste**

1. Preheat the oven to 375°.

2. Take out the little bag of innards from the chicken and set aside. Rinse off your bird, then put it in a cast-iron skillet (so you can make your gravy in the same pan when the chicken is done) and bake covered for 30 minutes.

3. Melt the butter in a small saucepan and mix in the onion, garlic, salt, and pepper.

4. Pour the butter mixture over the chicken, then put it back in the hot oven and cook uncovered for another 30 minutes, basting with the butter mixture at least twice. Let stand 5 minutes before carving. The chicken that comes out will be a dry, crispy little bird, which is the way I like it best. If you want it juicy and less crisp, then cover it the whole time it is cooking.

Serves 4

Chicken Gravy

Making good gravy is another wonderfully inexact Cracker science, but it can be boiled down to (pardon the pun) three basic elements: hot grease, flour, then, after a little stirring, the addition of liquid. All require your attention (hot grease always requires attention), but the third part is the tricky one. Add too much liquid, and you have thin gravy. Add too little, and it'll be too thick and will scorch. The best way to do it is over medium heat, adding the liquid slowly, so you'll see how thick or thin it'll be. Once you have the desired consistency, add spices and additions. If the liquid is any kind of dairy, take it very slowly, or you'll curdle your milk and your gravy will have little annoying flecks in it. I usually add a little water first to cool it down, then add the dairy. Then taste, adjust, consider, and re-spice if needed.

And don't worry if you ruin the gravy a few times. It's a natural part of the Cracker experience to burn, curdle, overspice, or generally fail in a culinary pursuit. Just toss the failure to the dogs, then tell everyone as you sit at the table, "Rernt the gravy."

If they're True Crackers, they won't challenge you or ask for details. They'll be too busy fighting for a drumstick to let a little gravy hold them back.

Drippings from 1 roasted chicken
2 tablespoons salted butter
2 tablespoons plain flour
¼ cup water
1 cup whole milk or sour cream
1 tablespoon soy sauce
½ teaspoon seasoning salt
½ teaspoon ground black pepper
1 clove garlic, crushed through a
       press

1. When your chicken is finished baking, remove it from the skillet. Heat the drippings with the butter over medium-high heat till melted.

2. Sprinkle in the flour and whisk as it cooks till it is a medium-brown color.

3. Add the water and whisk until smooth. Gradually whisk in enough milk to make the gravy thicken to the right consistency. Add the soy sauce, salt, pepper, and garlic.

4. Turn off the heat and stir till well blended.

Makes 2 cups

Chicken Perloo

Perloo is basically Cracker Chicken and Rice and is known in flashier parts of the South as pilau or pilaf. It is another mainstay of church suppers and funerals and, as always, has many delectable variations. You can give it a Louisiana flavor by adding 2 cups chopped okra and a can of stewed tomatoes, or make it a glorified yellow rice by substituting a commercially packaged yellow rice for the brown rice. If you want it to be truly delicious, then use a hen instead of a lowly chicken. For the truly uninitiated, a hen is a lady chicken of a certain age, and like mature women everywhere, she is curvy and succulent and full of rich flavor. If I were poultry, I'd be a hen. They rule the roost and make the best chicken stock. If you're cooking for prospective in-laws or a really hot date, then pay a couple more bucks for a fat hen.

Old-school Crackers served their perloo with chicken pieces on top and rice on the bottom, but if you're serving children or lazy relatives, you can bone the chicken before you put it back in the rice in step 4.

¼ cup sweet butter
2 cups chopped Vidalia onion
1 cup diced celery
2 tablespoons minced garlic
1½ cups diced green bell pepper
¼ teaspoon red pepper flakes
1 chicken or hen, 3 to 4 pounds, quartered
4 cups chicken stock or canned broth
2 cups brown rice
Salt and ground black pepper to taste
(heavy on the pepper)
½ teaspoon curry powder
Several dashes of hot sauce

1. Brown the butter in a large pot over medium-high heat. Add the onion, celery, garlic, bell pepper, and pepper flakes and sauté for 4 to 5 minutes, till the vegetables are limp and chewy.

2. Add the chicken pieces skin side down and cook over medium heat for 5 minutes, till the skin is browned. Increase the heat to medium-high, add the stock, and cook for 10 minutes, till the chicken is almost done. Hens are fatter than chickens, so if you're doing a hen, add another 10 minutes to the process.

3. Remove the chicken pieces from the broth, then add the rice, salt and pepper, curry, and hot sauce. Cover and slowly simmer for 40 minutes, till the liquid is mostly absorbed and your house smells heavenly of onions and garlic.

4. Put the chicken on top of the rice mixture and simmer covered for another 5 minutes. Turn off the heat and let steam for another 5 minutes.

Serves 5

Chinatown Chicken Almond

This fine little recipe is a fairly recent addition to Cracker cuisine, dating back twenty years, when Burger first introduced it to me at a church supper. I call it a Cracker recipe because she is an Alabama Corn Cracker and is married to a fourth-generation Ft. Ogden Cracker (whose family moved to Florida back when berries and salted venison were big items on the menu). Therefore anything that comes out of her kitchen is, in fact, a Cracker recipe, and proof positive that we are an evolving fusion culture. The apple juice makes it wonderfully tangy and good served over brown rice.

¼ **cup olive oil**

4 boneless, skinless chicken breast halves

2 tablespoons plain flour

¾ **cup apple juice**

¼ **cup soy sauce**

2 cups sliced mushrooms

Salt and ground black pepper to taste

2 ounces sliced almonds

1. Heat the oil in a large saucepan over medium heat. Add the chicken and brown on all sides. Remove the chicken to a cutting board and cut into bite-sized chunks. Return the chicken to the pan.

2. Put the flour, apple juice, and soy sauce in a measuring cup and mix well with a spoon. Pour it into the pan with the chicken and cook, stirring, over medium heat for 5 minutes.

3. Add the mushrooms and cook for 15 minutes, till the chicken is tender and the sauce is thickened. Season with salt and pepper to taste.

4. Spread the almonds on a cookie sheet and toast under the broiler for 1 minute or less (careful not to scorch), then fold into the chicken mixture.

Serves 4

White Beans and Ham

Beans are almost as good a traveling food as chicken and a particular staple in Cracker Cooking because they can be dried and eaten later. In the long days before refrigeration, this was a great asset for any food and particularly welcome to Cracker cowmen, who lived outdoors and cooked many stews over fires. There is so much ham flavor in this old classic that even the staunchest meat eater among us can eat it with cornbread and call himself full. It provides a little variety at funerals that are heavy on the fried chicken.

One 16-ounce package dried white beans
8 cups water
Large ham bone with some meat still on it,
> **or ½ cup diced ham**
½ teaspoon salt, if desired (the ham will
> **make it a little salty)**
1 tablespoon ground black pepper
1 clove garlic

1. Rinse the dried beans, then soak overnight in enough water to cover (if you forget, you can do the quick-boil method printed on the package).

2. When you're ready to cook, pour off the soaking water, then put the beans in a big pot with 8 cups water, the ham bone, salt, pepper, and garlic. Bring to a boil over medium-high heat.

3. Boil for 3 minutes, then turn down the heat and simmer covered for 1 hour, till the beans are tender to the point of bursting.

4. If you like creamier beans, squash a few with a spoon against the side of the pot.

Serves 8

Sweet Potato Pie

Sweet potatoes are favorites of Crackers for the same reason they're favorites of poor folk everywhere: They're easy to grow, plentiful, and can be seasoned (that is, preserved in straw) all winter, meaning that you never have to go to bed hungry as long as you have so much as a single sweet potato left. I'm offering two versions of the pie: one traditional, and a newer, creamier version, courtesy of the modern Cracker's recent infatuation with cream cheese (an affection that might one day equal, or even overtake, our love of the lowly hog).

Both versions are really scrumptious when topped with sweet whipped cream and a few chopped pecans. Eat with coffee at home, or bring to a funeral and send a good message—the departed was a person worth peeling sweet potatoes over.

1 pound fresh sweet potatoes
½ cup sweet butter, softened
1 cup sugar
One 12-ounce can evaporated milk
2 large eggs
Pinch of ground nutmeg
Larger pinch of ground cinnamon
2 teaspoons vanilla extract
One 9-inch Flaky Pie Crust (page 258)

1. Preheat the oven to 325°.

2. Bake the sweet potatoes whole for 40 to 50 minutes, until done, then dip in cold water. This makes removing the skins easier. Skin your potatoes.

3. Put the skinned potatoes in a large mixer bowl and squash with a potato masher. Add the butter, sugar, milk, eggs, nutmeg, cinnamon, and vanilla; beat the mixture until smooth.

4. Pour the mixture into the unbaked pie crust. Bake for about 1 hour, till a knife stuck in the middle comes out clean.

5. Cool before serving.

Serves 5

Sweet Potato Cream Pie

This pie is what happens when you leave a cheesecake and a sweet potato pie alone in the refrigerator overnight, unchaperoned: the midnight tryst, the tearful confession, and nine months later, the pitter-patter of a new little pie around the house. In this case, it is a happy accident. Birth dates and wedding anniversaries are adjusted and no one is ever the wiser.

> **One 8-ounce package cream cheese, softened**
> **1 cup mashed cooked sweet potato**
> **½ cup packed light brown sugar**
> **¼ cup granulated sugar**
> **1 tablespoon plain flour**
> **½ teaspoon ground cinnamon**
> **¼ teaspoon salt**
> **2 large eggs**
> **1 tablespoon vanilla extract**
> **Graham Cracker Crust (page 259)**

1. Preheat the oven to 350°.

2. Put the cream cheese, sweet potato, and both sugars in a large mixer bowl, then beat till smooth.

3. Blend in the flour, cinnamon, and salt. Add the eggs and vanilla and beat till blended.

4. Pour the mixture into the pie crust. Bake for 40 minutes, till firm.

5. Cool before slicing.

Serves 5

IV. SUNDAY DINNER

The secret to a good Sunday dinner is to find recipes that can be made ahead of time, and all of these can except for the beef, which will be slowly roasting while you nourish your soul (or if you're unchurched, while you work in an early round of golf or trim your hedges).

I'm beginning with a cheap pot roast, beloved of mid-century Cracker mothers thanks to its economy and ease in preparation. If chicken is the holy bird, chuck roast is the holy roast. When I was growing up, my mother would slowly bake a chuck or rump roast every Sunday while we were at church, making for a truly inspiring return home to a house scented with cooked garlic and onion and beef. The common theory was that Baptist services only went till twelve o'clock because the preachers were slaves to their deacon boards and they daren't burn anyone's roast.

Pot Roast and Vegetables

This practical little roast is designed for slow cooking. The bulbs of garlic will provide inner seasoning, and the water will steam up and make this basically cheap cut of beef a whole lot tenderer than you thought you'd get for $2.39 a pound. It makes for a complete dinner in a pan and is especially good with Miss Katie B's rolls.

One 5-pound eye-of-round beef roast
5 cloves garlic, peeled
2 big yellow onions, quartered
8 large carrots, peeled and cut into 2-inch pieces
8 medium red potatoes, peeled and quartered
2 stalks celery, cut into 2-inch pieces
1 cup water
Salt and ground black pepper to taste

1. Preheat the oven to 250°.

2. Put the roast in a roasting pan large enough to hold the roast and vegetables. Jab the roast five times with a knife, 1 inch deep, and insert a garlic clove into each incision.

3. Surround the roast with the onions, carrots, potatoes, and celery, then pour in the water and dust with salt and pepper.

4. Cover the pan with a lid or aluminum foil. Cook in the oven for 2 hours, time for Sunday school and church unless you have a long-winded preacher.

5. Take the pan out of the oven and let stand for 5 minutes before carving the roast.

Serves 8 to 10

Strawberry-Pretzel Salad

Thanks to the strawberry growers of central Florida, the strawberry has made great inroads into mainstream Cracker cooking, and this salad recipe demonstrates how. It is salty, crunchy, sweet, and creamy. It is everything. I can't think of a meal that wouldn't be improved upon by the addition of this modest little fruit and cheesecake dish. It can be made ahead of time and chilled, to be later brought out in triumph with the roast.

2 cups crushed pretzels

¾ cup sweet butter, melted

3 tablespoons granulated sugar

One 8-ounce package cream cheese, softened

1 cup powdered sugar

2 cups whipped topping

One 6-ounce package strawberry gelatin

2 cups boiling water

2 cups cooked sweetened fresh strawberries, or
one 10-ounce bag frozen strawberries, thawed
and drained

1. Preheat the oven to 350°.

2. Mix together the pretzels, butter, and granulated sugar in a medium bowl, then press the mixture over the bottom of a 9 x 13-inch baking dish. Bake for 10 minutes, then remove and let cool.

3. Beat together the cream cheese, powdered sugar, and whipped topping in a medium mixing bowl and set aside.

4. Make the gelatin according to package directions with the boiling water. Add the strawberries and chill till the mixture is no longer hot but not yet set.

5. By now, the pretzel crust should be cool. To assemble the salad, spoon the cream cheese mixture in the crust, then add the slightly jelled strawberry mixture on top.

6. Chill for 1 hour, or even overnight, till set. Cut into squares and serve as salad or even dessert.

Makes about 22 squares

Wilted Country Salad

The beauty of this old-school Cracker salad is that it is supposed to be wilted, so there are no worries if the sermons go long. You don't have to worry your salad will lose its bounce.

2 heads leaf lettuce
6 green onions, thinly sliced
5 tablespoons cider vinegar
1 tablespoon sugar
1 teaspoon salt
¼ teaspoon ground black pepper
6 strips thick-sliced bacon, cooked till crisp

1. Rinse the lettuce, dry, and tear into bite-sized pieces.

2. Combine the onions, vinegar, sugar, salt, and pepper in a medium pan and simmer over low heat for 2 minutes, till the sugar is dissolved. Turn off the heat and stir in the cooked bacon to make a light dressing.

3. Just before serving, pour the hot dressing over the lettuce and toss.

Serves 4

Pecan Pie

No Southern cookbook is complete without a shout-out to this old-time favorite, Pecan Pie. This version is sometimes called blonde pecan pie and is closely akin to the recipe that appeared on the label of Karo corn syrup for time out of mind. I swear it's been around so long it's part of the Alabama SATs. It is good served warm with a scoop of vanilla ice cream.

2 large eggs
1 cup white corn syrup
¼ cup sugar
2 tablespoons plain flour
1 tablespoon vanilla extract
1 cup whole pecans, chopped
One 9-inch Flaky Pie Crust (page 258)

1. Preheat the oven to 350°.
2. Whisk the eggs together in a large mixing bowl. Add the corn syrup, sugar, flour, and vanilla and mix well.
3. Put the pecans in the bottom of the unbaked pie shell, then pour the syrup mixture over the pecans.
4. Bake for 1 hour, until a knife inserted in the center comes out clean.
5. Cool before serving.

Serves 6

V. MOTHER'S DAY

MENU

Mama's Fried Chicken

Fried Chicken Tenderloins

Vegetable Beef Soup

Grannie's Chicken and Dumplings

Light-and-Easy Chicken and Dumplings

Potato Salad

Peach Cobbler

You might be surprised at the list of recipes above, which are random and heavy on the chicken, but these Mother's Day dishes aren't so much a menu as they are a list of great, time-honored favorites handed down to me by my own mother, Martha Rice Johnson, and my grandmother, Eula Roberts Rice. I offer them in their honor. The first is Mama's old-school version of fried chicken. It's heavy on the pepper and capable of lifting you from the deepest hole of despair.

I'm not exaggerating either. I almost died after the birth of my middle daughter, Abby, of complications and sepsis that gave me a raging, week-long fever and was only cured by emergency surgery that saved my Cracker life. I was so sick that I was hallucinating. When I finally got through it and came home, Mama was staying with the baby. She not only cooked me a homecoming supper but also rearranged my whole dang house. I remember just laying there in bed, weirdly disjointed from real life, wondering how my house had come to be so blindingly clean and why it smelled so strongly of Pine-Sol. I was too weak to grasp the obvious—that Mama had cleaned up. I just lay there, looking around, till she appeared at the door with my supper (the same thing she used to make me when I was sick when I was a child): fried chicken, buttered rice, and a homemade biscuit with tomato gravy. All were peppered and buttered to perfection, and along with a glass of her iced tea, they restored me completely. When I was done, I sat up in bed in a considerably brighter mood, smelling the Pine-Sol and praying that I'd be as good a mother to Abby as my mother was to me. I pray it still.

Here's a recent photo from the family shoebox that illustrates our hope for the future better than words ever could: a snapshot of Mama holding her first great-grandbaby, the utterly wonderful and unmatchable Lily P. The picture was taken while Mama was telling one of her old stories about Grannie or Granddaddy or Uncle Kelly and Aunt Doris, or someone she grew up with at church.

If you still haven't grasped the soul of the species *Crackus Americanis,* take a long look at her face. It is the face of an angel.

Kathy Haven Cutler

Mama's Fried Chicken

I must confess that this is really just an approximation of Mama's famous fried chicken—approximate because my mother has never looked at a recipe in her life and gets a brain freeze when you ask her how to make her Martha Classics. This is my version and it is very close, heavy on pepper and garlic salt and really not much else, as Mama has never gone for the Colonel's seven secret spices, or whatever they used to call it. Her version is better than mine because she has no compunction about frying in lard, and I've been polluted by all those articles on how lard's the devil, so I usually fry mine in peanut or canola oil. You can decide if your arteries can handle the original. If not, use peanut oil, which heats well. To be fair and balanced, I'll add a few minor adjustments that will produce a slightly healthier plate of fried chicken.

5 cups self-rising flour
1 teaspoon ground black pepper
1 teaspoon garlic salt
½ teaspoon paprika
½ teaspoon dried rosemary
One 3-pound chicken, cut up at the joints
2 large eggs, beaten
2 pounds lard

1. Put the dry ingredients in a deep bowl and stir till blended.

2. Roll each piece of chicken in the beaten eggs, then turn in the flour mixture till well coated.

3. Heat the lard in a cast-iron Dutch oven till it's hot but not smoking. Carefully drop in the chicken pieces, three pieces at a time.

4. Fry for 5 minutes on one side, then put on the lid and fry for a minute or two. Turn over the chicken with tongs, careful not to pierce the skin, then fry uncovered on the other side for 3 minutes, till the crust is golden brown.

5. Take out the chicken with tongs and add the next three pieces. Take your time, or you'll crowd the pan and get a soggy crust.

6. When you're finished frying, let the chicken cool on a platter large enough for each piece not to touch. As it cools, the crust will get ever more crunchy, till ecstasy stage, when you sit down and eat.

Serves 4

Fried Chicken Tenderloins

My daughters are young Metro Crackers, who insist on a few lower-calorie versions of our old family favorites. Here we are, en famille, at Em's UF graduation dinner at a local sushi restaurant, and a more up-market table of Crackers you'll never find.

This recipe for chicken tenderloins is slightly healthier than the preceding since it's fried without skin in canola oil.

4 cups self-rising flour

1 teaspoon seasoning salt

½ teaspoon ground black pepper

½ teaspoon garlic powder

½ teaspoon paprika

½ teaspoon dried rosemary

2 pounds chicken tenderloins

1 large egg, beaten

3 cups canola oil

Follow the directions for Mama's Fried Chicken (recipe precedes). The tenderloins will fry much quicker, about 2 minutes on each side.

Serves 6

Vegetable Beef Soup

My mother's soup is cheap and wonderfully packed with tomatoes and will simmer quietly in a Crock-Pot all day if you're at work or out of the house. Stews and soups are by definition a variation waiting to happen, and this one is no exception. I sometimes toss corn into this, or chopped green peppers, or really anything else I happen to have in the garden or the house that is fresh and tangy. It is another one of those modest-sounding little dishes that will worm its way into your heart, and the hearts of your children. Feed them this when they're young, and when they're old, they'll sit around the fire and tell their grandchildren about their old Mama's soup. What a soup that was!

2 tablespoons canola oil
2 pounds beef stew meat, cut into 1-inch
      pieces
2 teaspoons plain flour
4 cups cold water
1 rib celery, chopped
1 large yellow onion, chopped
Two 10-ounce cans stewed tomatoes
4 white potatoes, peeled and chopped
2 carrots, peeled and cut into 1-inch pieces
1 bay leaf
Dash of hot sauce
Salt and lots of ground black pepper to taste

1. Heat the oil in a cast-iron Dutch oven over medium-high heat. Add the stew meat, in batches if necessary, and brown on all sides.

2. Sprinkle with the flour and stir. Cook the roux till medium brown.

3. Turn down the heat to medium-low. Add the water, vegetables, and seasonings.

4. Simmer covered for 2 hours, till the vegetables are tender, or in a slow cooker all day on the low setting.

5. Fish out the bay leaf and discard before serving.

Serves 5

Here is another classic shot from Mama's shoebox of photographs. (Why scrapbook when you can shoebox?) The sweet old Cracker couple is Grannie and Granddaddy, holding my cousin Steve. You might note that Grannie is holding in her stomach for the shot. When you see her recipe for chicken and dumplings, you'll know why.

She needn't have worried on my account as there was no one on earth I loved more than my grannie, who taught me the fine art of storytelling. Like many a young Crackerling before me, I shared a bed and bedroom with my Grannie, and every night of my childhood, she'd end my day with a story—Aesop's fables and Bible stories, and endless recollections from her past. She was born Baptist in southern Alabama and became Pentecostal when she moved to Florida, because there wasn't a convenient Baptist Church on the west end of Marianna. She was quickly filled with the Holy Ghost and forever thereafter was a certified Saved, Holy-Ghost-filled, Water-baptized, Jesus-on-my-mind kind of Christian. My granddaddy, who was a son of the infamous uber-Cracker Rice clan of Floyd County, Georgia, didn't share her enthusiasm but could be best described as colorful and, well, *earthy* might be a suitable adjective. They married when Grannie was nineteen and he was a well-heeled thirty-four-year-old sawyer at the local heading mill in Sumter County, Alabama.

They were a devoted couple till their dying day, their only parting of minds over

Grannie's devotion to the holiness church, which Granddaddy shared not at all. The funniest story about this famous split of sensibility happened after the war, when the L&N railroad went from coal to electric. Their house in Marianna was built right on the edge of the railroad embankment. When the new electric engine came roaring down the tracks in the middle of the night with the whistle blaring and the light flashing, Grannie woke up with a start and shouted, "Wake up, Ike! Jesus is coming!" to which Granddaddy replied in tones of great Cracker disgust (Mama heard him through the wall), "*Shit,* Euler."

It pretty much encapsulates the myth and the magic of Ike and Eula and the threads of heaven and earth woven through the fabric of our old Cracker life.

Grannie's Chicken and Dumplings

There are many versions of chicken and dumplings, and I'm providing two: old-school and light. The dish is a Cracker favorite for a lot of reasons, economy not the least, as most Cracker homesteads had a flock of chickens pecking around the yard and a cook who could ring a chicken's neck in two-seconds flat and pluck it even faster. If you've ever watched a Cracker woman take on a chicken, it goes something like this: Grab, click, and yank, yank, yank; after a flurry of feathers, a naked little bird emerges.

If you're of Italian persuasion, you'll notice that dumplings are really just fat noodles cooked in a bubbling preparation of chicken, stock, and whatever else floats your boat. I sometimes throw in dried onions or green onions or soy sauce or any other spice I see when I open up my cabinet. The lighter version is quick and easy and could easily be made fat free without the inclusion of my usual chunk of butter.

Test, taste, and ponder. Make it your own.

BROTH

1 chicken or hen, about 4 pounds

3 small yellow onions, chopped

3 cups water

One 10-ounce can condensed chicken broth

2 teaspoons ground sea salt

½ teaspoon ground black pepper

½ teaspoon dried rosemary

2 bay leaves

¼ teaspoon dried thyme

2 tablespoons fresh lemon juice

1. First decide on your basic bird. The cheapest, most common these days are the little chickens you buy sealed in plastic, whole or cut up. They're cheap, but it's aggravating to pick out the bones, so decide how much work you're willing to do before choosing your bird: canned and boned (and not as good) or the whole bird (better).

Lately Tyson and all the big chicken people offer bags of breast and tenders, all ready to toss in the pot. They're skinless, so brace yourself for the difference, but, hey, it's still chicken.

2. Put whatever chicken you choose in a big pot and add the onions, water, and broth. If you like the livers, stick them in, too, but do warn everyone in advance. I myself am not a fan. Add the salt, pepper, rosemary, bay leaves, thyme, and lemon juice.

3. Cook uncovered over low heat till the chicken falls apart completely. Let it cool, then set yourself the task of picking out all them dang bones, and there are a lot of them. When you're done, fish out the bay leaves and return the chicken to the pot. Make your dumplings.

DUMPLINGS

2 cups plain flour, plus 1 cup for rolling out
1 teaspoon salt
⅓ cup vegetable shortening, softened
½ cup whole milk

1. Put 2 cups flour in a large bowl and blend in the salt.

2. Cut in the shortening with a fork or pastry blender (just as you do a pie crust).

3. Stir in enough of the milk to make a soft dough and shape it into a ball.

4. Sprinkle your countertop with another cup of flour. Roll out the dough ⅛ inch thick with either a rolling pin or a round glass. Cut into roughly 2 x 2-inch squares (or just pinch them off before rolling the dough if you like, into whatever shape fits your fork).

5. Bring the pot of chicken and stock to a low boil. Slowly drop the dumplings into the broth, making sure each one is submerged a moment before you put in the next one, or they'll stick together.

6. Cook over medium heat for 10 minutes, stirring occasionally to make sure they don't stick. Cover the pot, turn off the heat, and let them set for a few minutes to mix and mingle and get to know each other.

7. Some people like this dish dry (with dumplings that stick together) and some like it soupy. You decide which way you like it and add a little water to make it soupier if that's what you like.

Serves 6

Light-and-Easy
Chicken and Dumplings

For all you lazy Crackers, here is the modern shortcut I use quite a bit. It doesn't have the mule-kick glory of the real Grannie item, but it's warm and cozy on a cold night. If you liven it up with spices and soy, then it comes out pretty good and edible, but if you're really looking for comfort, add ¼ cup butter. I usually do, but I don't tell anyone because the fat you don't know about doesn't count. It's my secret ingredient and allows my skinny girls to eat these dumplings without guilt but with great pleasure; plus, it cements my reputation as a legendary cook. When I'm dead and gone and they're eating other fat-free versions of chicken and dumplings, they will shrug and say, "This is all right, but something about the way Mama made it—rich, creamy. It really stuck with you, and it was fat-free, by gosh! How *did* she do it?"

Which is as fine a legacy as any Cracker mother could ask.

I usually serve my chicken and dumplings with pole beans or fresh tomatoes on a plate with sliced sweet onions and sprinkled with pepper and salt. Add pie for dessert and present it to any prospective suitor. If they don't kneel down and kiss your feet when they're done, or at least ask you to marry them, then move on to the next prospect. The first one obviously wasn't worth your time.

One 32-ounce can chicken broth
1 cup water
½ teaspoon dried rosemary
1 bay leaf
2 tablespoons dried minced onion
1 teaspoon salt
1 teaspoon ground black pepper
1 pound frozen chicken tenders, thawed and
    cut into 1-inch pieces
1 tablespoon soy sauce

**One 12-ounce bag frozen dumplings (in frozen food
    case by frozen biscuits; if you can't find
    them, use wide egg noodles)**
¼ cup sweet butter (optional)

1. Combine the chicken broth, water, rosemary, bay leaf, onion, salt, pepper, chicken tenders, and soy sauce in a large saucepan and cook over medium-high heat for 10 minutes.

2. Add the dumplings and cook as directed on the package, usually 10 to 15 minutes, stirring to make sure they don't stick.

3. When the dumplings thicken, stir them around till the tenders fall apart. Stir in the butter.

Serves 5

Potato Salad

This is another Mama favorite: a standard potato salad recipe, sans mustard, which can be made in advance. It's popular with the dinner-on-the-grounds set and is the classic Cracker side for fried chicken.

Actually, it's pretty dang good with anything.

6 large white potatoes, peeled and
    chopped into 1-inch pieces
3 large eggs
½ large sweet onion, chopped
¼ cup chopped dill pickles
⅔ cup mayonnaise
½ teaspoon prepared horseradish
1 tablespoon vinegar from pickle jar
Salt and ground black pepper to taste

1. Boil the potatoes in a big pot of water over medium-high heat for 10 minutes. Add the whole eggs and cook another 5 minutes. Turn off the heat, put on the lid, and let cool on the stovetop.

2. While the potatoes are cooling, combine the remaining ingredients in a large bowl and toss till well mixed.

3. Drain the potatoes and add to the mayonnaise mixture. Peel and chop the eggs and add them. Mix well.

4. Cover and chill if you prefer your potato salad cold. If you like it warm, then put it all together just before serving.

Serves 6

Peach Cobbler

Grannie and Aunt Izzy were fond of making cobbler, which was cheap and easy and used up some of those canned peaches and pears they'd put up the summer before. This recipe is well known and can be made with any fruit: blueberries, blackberries, peaches, and so on.

The secret is to let the butter lay there in the bottom of the pan when you pour in the batter and to resist the urge to stir. Just let the hot butter do its work below, while the peaches carry the top. Serve with vanilla ice cream, while it's still warm.

1 cup sliced fresh peaches, blueberries,
cherries, or what have you
1¾ cups sugar, divided
½ cup sweet butter
¾ cup self-rising flour
⅔ cup buttermilk

STREUSEL TOPPING
3 tablespoons sweet butter, softened
2 cups brown sugar
3 tablespoons plain flour
3 tablespoons finely chopped pecans

1. Preheat the oven to 400°.

2. Put the fruit in a medium mixing bowl and cover with 1 cup of the sugar. Stir well and set aside.

3. Melt the butter in a deep casserole in the oven.

4. Mix the remaining ¾ cup sugar, the flour, and buttermilk in a mixing bowl until smooth.

5. Pour the batter over the butter, without stirring, then top with the fruit.

6. To make the topping, cut the butter into the sugar and flour with a fork till crumbly and add the pecans. Sprinkle over the fruit.

7. Bake the cobbler for 30 minutes. Turn off the oven and leave the cobbler in the oven for an additional 20 minutes, till brown.

Serves 6

CHAPTER TWO

They Don't Call Them Dog Days for Nothing

Summer in the South used to be an ordeal to be endured, though old-timers claim it wasn't as hot before the invention of the air conditioner, or at least it didn't feel as hot. They say you'd get used to the heat and work your life around it. In Florida, Cracker farmers would rise long before dawn and do their chores and field work till ten or eleven in the morning, when they'd retire to eat lunch and sit on their porch, hat over their faces, and take a long nap. Around four, they'd bestir themselves and return to the field and labor till dark. To try to work through the hot part of the day was to chance a case of heat stroke, or heat exhaustion, which went by names such as *bear-caught* or *white-eyed*. If someone looked to be going white-eyed, they were drenched in water or pulled to the shade, as it could kill you as quick as a rattlesnake bite. They also drank a lot of cool water, or ice water if they could get it. At the end of a long day, they would feel like princes as they sat on the porch and felt the cool night breeze on their faces, claiming it was altogether more satisfying than artificially cooled air.

Modern Crackers have inherited their love of a cool breeze, and Memorial Day marks the beginning of the great summer outdoor season, with regular trips to the Lake or the Springs ("the Sprangs," we call them around here). It is the season of abundant fresh seafood and the cheap and plentiful produce that comes early in North Florida and is sold on every corner.

I'm starting with the holidays and ending with a selection of summer vegetable classics that are now pretty much available year round. Mix and match and cook a supper of them with some Cracklin' Cornbread on the side. The cracklin's will give you the prerequisite pork, and people won't murmur behind your back that you've become a vegetarian and a liberal.

I. MEMORIAL DAY

MENU

Barbara's Barbecued Shrimp

Baked Cheese Grits

Carrot-Raisin Salad

Peanut Butter Pie

●

Since Crackers are both sentimental and patriotic, Memorial Day is the perfect kick-off to a long and carefree summer. This charming little holiday comes right on the tail end of the school year and marks the official flag-flying season. Bright and early in the morning, Crackers go out, blow off their front yard, and unroll their American flag, flying it from a balcony, porch, or second-story window. It is hung in memory of all the hero ancestors we've lost in battle and marks the official start of the barefoot, beer-sipping, sand-in-your-underwear summer. For two-and-a-half glorious months no one has to buy heating oil, or wake up early to get their children to the car pool, or wear shoes that require socks. Unless you're a softball parent, you won't even have to mold your life around a sport schedule. For a few glorious weeks here, from late May till early football sign-ups, you'll be blessedly free and can actually pursue a few passions of your own: plant a few tomatoes and listen to FM radio; pluck your eyebrows and seriously consider going blonde.

Viva la sunshine.

Barbara's Barbecued Shrimp

You'll start your Memorial Day off right with this fail-proof recipe that is light and seafood-y and destined to be a family classic. It was passed along by a friend of mine, Barbara C, who is a native of Blountstown, Florida, and might be called a Grand Duchess of the Species. It is her own signature recipe and can be easily doubled or even tripled, which Barbara does when she serves it to her large and illustrious family at big summer gatherings. Diners have to peel their own, as they say in the South, and they'll be happy to do it.

1 cup sweet butter
¾ tablespoon ground black pepper
1 tablespoon dried Italian seasoning
1 clove garlic, crushed through a garlic press
2 pounds unshelled medium shrimp (50 count)

1. Preheat the oven to 350°.

2. Melt the butter in a roasting pan. Add the seasonings and stir, then add the shrimp.

3. Cover and bake for 20 to 30 minutes. Serve with French bread to dip in the sauce.

Serves 4 to 6

Baked Cheese Grits

Ah, the lowly grit, that versatile, lovable old Cracker favorite that (people tell me) is hard to find outside the South. I've only been above the Mason-Dixon once in my life (and only for a day), so I wouldn't know about their scarcity, but I can give you a hint as to their popularity in the Cracker past. Grits are hot; they are abundant, and they will by-gosh stick to your ribs. Give your farmhands (that is, your children) cold cereal for breakfast and see how many rows they hoe. Make them a pot of grits and butter, and they'll hoe till dinner and be glad to do it. It is a fortifying grain, and originally not a breakfast food at all but a whole meal in itself. It is as delicious as it is filling as long as you obey our family credo and put in a ratio of 70 percent grits and 30 percent butter, and salt it while it's cooking, or it isn't fit to feed the hogs. Restaurants often err in this manner and get many a dark look from their Cracker patrons, who aren't too thrilled with paying $2 for a nickel bowl of grits anyway. If you're the unlucky waitress who serves them, forget the tip. Just hope they left their firearms in the truck.

Here is a simple basic recipe for baked cheese grits that can be heated up with a few chopped peppers, if you're looking for a little color and zest. Even without them, this is a zesty variation, with a dash of hot sauce that will give your grits a pleasing orange tint and a little bite. If you add peppers, set aside a milder version for the young'uns and the womenfolk (including me).

4 cups whole milk

2 cups water

1½ cups fast-cooking grits (usually in the oatmeal aisle at the grocery store)

1½ cups shredded sharp Cheddar cheese, divided

⅓ cup sweet butter

3 large eggs, beaten

1 teaspoon salt

½ teaspoon ground black pepper, or to taste

1 tablespoon finely chopped serrano or jalapeño peppers (optional)

1 teaspoon hot sauce

1. Preheat the oven to 350°.

2. Put the milk and water in a deep saucepan and heat over high heat to boiling. Add the grits. Cook, stirring, till they are just below boiling. Reduce the heat and simmer uncovered till thickened.

3. Stir in 1 cup of the cheese, the butter, eggs, salt, and pepper. If you want your grits colorful and a little hot, stir in the peppers and hot sauce.

4. Pour into a buttered 9 x 13-inch baking dish. Bake for 30 minutes.

5. Take the dish out of the oven and sprinkle with the remaining ½ cup cheese.

Serves 8

Carrot-Raisin Salad

Back in the day when Morrison's had a buffet in every little Southern village on earth, my mother would order the same dang thing every time we went: trout almandine and a variation on this sweet little carrot-raisin salad. I have no recipe for the trout, but I do have one for a similar salad, which has color and texture and creamy pizzazz.

2 cups coarsely grated peeled carrots
1 tablespoon fresh lemon juice
½ cup dark raisins
⅓ cup mayonnaise
1 tablespoon sugar

1. Combine all the ingredients in a medium bowl and mix till well blended.
2. Chill for at least 1 hour and stir before serving.

Serves 6

Peanut Butter Pie

This summer pie is a light version of cheesecake and is requested so often by my nephews and daughters' roommates that it has become an Owens house classic. I've done many variations, but the chocolate on top and chocolate crust is the prizewinner.

CRUST

> **20 chocolate sandwich cookies, crushed**
> **¼ cup sweet butter, melted**
> **1 tablespoon sugar**

1. Preheat the oven to 325°.

2. Put the cookies in a plastic freezer bag and crush them with the heavy end of a tumbler, a meat pounder, or a regular old hammer.

3. Mix the crushed cookies, butter, and sugar in a mixing bowl, then press the mixture into a 9-inch pie plate, covering the bottom and the sides.

4. Bake for 10 minutes. Let cool for 20 minutes before filling.

FILLING

> **One 8-ounce package cream cheese, softened**
> **1 cup peanut butter**
> **1 cup powdered sugar**
> **One 12-ounce tub whipped topping, thawed**
> **2 ounces dark chocolate, grated**

1. Beat the cream cheese, peanut butter, sugar, and whipped topping in a mixer bowl till smooth and blended.

2. Spoon the mixture into the cooled cookie crust and smooth the top, then top with the grated chocolate.

Serves 6

II. FOURTH OF JULY

Grilled Sausages

Grilled Corn on the Cob

Grilled Bourbon Chicken Wings

Cranberry Waldorf Salad

Fourth of July Flag Cake

Banana Split Cake

Iced Tea *(page 252)*

Soft drinks and beer

Hurrah for the Land of the Free.

Never in the history of the world have any conquered people celebrated the birthday of their oppressors as Crackers do the Fourth of July. We let bygones be bygones and do the fireworks, go to the springs, jet ski around the lake, and even pull out the old grill for a smoking good time.

I call the early patriots "oppressors" with tongue-in-cheek, as the fact of the matter is that this Cracker has at least seven verified patriots in her direct ancestral line, and the early patriot credo *live free or die* could be said to sum up the Cracker American experience. Just because their hardheaded Confederate grandsons would eventually have a bone to pick with the Federalists, which resulted in their seceding from the union, their grandfathers' sacrifices to birth this nation cannot go unnoticed. So, again, I say: Hurrah for the Land of the Free.

Grilled Sausages

Sausage grills well, though it requires careful watching so it doesn't flame up and burn. In my book, a little singe is okay. We split our sausages before we cook them. I know some folks argue that splitting them drains the flavor, but it also drains some of the fat. If they're homemade, there's probably more than enough fat to drain.

3 pounds large link sausages: country, kielbasas,
   bratwursts, or what have you

1. Heat the grill to a low, steady heat—low gas or simmering coals.

2. Split the sausages, lay them out on a hot part of the grill, and watch that the draining fat doesn't ignite the flames (or you'll have charred sausage).

3. Grill them for 3 to 5 minutes on each side, till bubbling brown.

Serves 6

Grilled Corn on the Cob

Grilling corn in the husk makes the chef's job a little easier and the eater's job a little more challenging. I've always thought that nature provided a nice little browning bag right there with the husk, and I use it whenever I can.

12 ears sweet corn, still in their husks
Melted butter
Salt and freshly ground black pepper

1. Peel off the outside layers and all the silk from the corn but leave a few layers of husk.

2. Soak the corn in its thinned-out husk encasings in water for 10 minutes to produce a nice little head of steam while you're roasting them.

3. Shake off the extra water. When your grill is hot, put them on as you would lay out hamburger patties, taking care to move them around occasionally to make sure they're all evenly hot.

4. Grill for 15 minutes over medium-high heat. Serve the corn in the husks for guests to rip off and apply their own butter, salt, and pepper to the corn. If you can't serve the corn right away, wrap it in aluminum foil to keep warm.

Makes 12 ears corn

Grilled Bourbon Chicken Wings

When you have a hot grill, throw on whatever is handy and use that energy while you've got it. These wings are perfect on the grill—not as devilishly hot as hot wings but a little on the sweet side. I realize that this recipe calls for brown sugar and some barbecue experts really frown on grilling sugar (as if it were the Eleventh Commandment), but I happen to like the caramelized taste of cooked sugar.

In any case, this recipe doesn't have enough sugar to do much damage and offers a mildly sweet garlic and bourbon flavor. The wings can be marinated overnight or for at least 2 hours.

> **24 chicken wings**
> **3 tablespoons bourbon**
> **3 tablespoons olive oil**
> **Juice of 1 lemon**
> **1 clove garlic, minced**
> **1 tablespoon brown sugar**
> **Salt and ground black pepper to taste**

1. Cut the wings into little joints and drumettes and discard the tips. Combine all the other ingredients in a large bowl. Add the wings and toss to coat. Marinate the wings in the mixture for at least 2 hours in the refrigerator.

2. Preheat your grill to medium-hot.

3. Cook the wings on the hot grill till crisp, about 5 minutes on each side.

Serves 4

Cranberry Waldorf Salad

This is another recipe from my best friend Burger's collection that is simply delicious and good for any kind of outdoor grilling session, as it can be made ahead and chilled till ready. I can get fresh or frozen cranberries year-round here in the deep South, so I assume everyone else in America can, too. Traditional Waldorf salad is made with walnuts—or so I hear. I prefer pecans; since they're cheap and abundant, my Cracker salad is made with our own native nut.

One 12-ounce package fresh cranberries
2 cups sugar
4 medium tart green apples
1 large bunch seedless grapes
½ cup chopped pecans
1 cup vanilla yogurt

1. Rinse and pick over the cranberries, then coarsely chop them in a food processor. Stir the sugar into the berries, cover, and chill for at least 4 hours.

2. Place the cranberries in a sieve and drain well—takes about 2 hours.

3. When the cranberries are drained, core and chop the apples. Combine the apples, grapes, nuts, and yogurt in a large bowl. Gently fold in the cranberries. Chill until ready to serve.

Serves 8 to 10

Fourth of July Flag Cake

Like the ever-popular Easter Bunny Cake, the Flag Cake is a favorite with the young'uns, who can be called on to provide the decoration. If you live in Alabama and leave a young'un to his own devices, you'll inevitably end up with Flag Cake in the design of Rebel stars and bars, so be forewarned.

It'll eat well, regardless.

1 box white cake mix
One 12-ounce tub whipped topping
One 8-ounce carton sour cream
1 tablespoon vanilla extract
1 cup powdered sugar
1 pint blueberries
1 pint strawberries, hulled
1 cup freshly shredded coconut

1. Preheat the oven to 325°.

2. Bake the cake according to package directions in a 9 x 13-inch pan. Let cool completely.

3. Mix the whipped topping and sour cream in a mixer bowl until well blended, then add the vanilla and sugar and beat until smooth.

4. When the cake is cool to the touch, frost it with the cream mixture. Make a flag design with the fruit, varying the blueberries for stars, the strawberries for red stripes, and the flaked coconut for the white ones.

5. Chill for at least 1 hour before serving.

Serves 6 to 8

Banana Split Cake

I remember the day my sister-in-law Jeana first introduced this memorable cake to the weekly Johnson cookout that my parents held every Saturday afternoon, from roughly '77 till I married in '80. We weren't celebrating anything in particular; we just had a regular little party mostly because we could. In time Jeana and I got into a small dessert competition, resulting in spectacular creations like this Banana Split Cake, which really isn't a cake as much as a layered, crunchy-crust wonder.

It doesn't require baking, so you won't have to heat up the house. If you're allergic to butter, you might want to have a paramedic on hand before you sit down to eat.

2 cups graham cracker crumbs
½ cup sweet butter, melted
2 large egg whites
2 cups powdered sugar
1 cup sweet butter, softened
6 bananas, peeled and halved lengthwise
One 20-ounce can (2½ cups) crushed pineapple, drained
1 quart strawberries, hulled and halved
One 16-ounce tub whipped topping, thawed
1 cup chopped pecans

1. Mix together the graham cracker crumbs and melted butter and press over the bottom of a 9 x 13-inch square baking pan. Refrigerate for 30 minutes.

2. Beat the egg whites in a large mixer bowl till fluffy. Add the powdered sugar, ½ cup at a time, and the softened butter and beat for 10 minutes, till the mixture is truly fluffy.

3. Spread the butter mixture over the crust. Top with the bananas in an even layer, then the pineapple, then the strawberries.

4. Spread the whipped topping over the fruit layers and sprinkle with the pecans.

5. Chill for 3 hours or overnight.

Serves 8

If you need more side dishes for any of your summer celebrations, jump ahead to the section on summer garden fare (page 100) to find even more salad and vegetable dishes to add to your feasts.

Here's a photo of Daddy's family posed around the table at a summer eat-a-thon in Phenix City, Alabama, circa 1958. On the far right is Uncle Howard, whose grandson Jamey Johnson is a bona fide country music star (he won best songwriter last year for George Straight's hit "Give It Away"). Jamey's daddy, Ronald, is the towhead to the side, diving into a slice of watermelon. You'll meet Jamey's uncle Johnny shortly, in the barbecue section. Uncle Grover weighs down the far end of the table, and a quick glance at my paternal gene pool here illustrates why I never have aspired to model thinness.

And let the record show that Big Mama (third from right, spitting out a watermelon seed) was considered uncommonly attractive in her day—a backwoods Marilyn Monroe—which makes me mighty nostalgic for that time in American history when a big-boned woman could have her pound cake and eat it, too.

III. LIGHT SUMMER SUPPER

Peppers and Steak

Broiled Cheesy Tomatoes

Cornpone or Corn Muffins

Homemade Brandied Peach Ice Cream

Iced Tea *(page 252)*

Peppers and Steak

The beauty of this light summer supper is that it's made mostly on the stovetop instead of in the oven, so it doesn't heat up the house. You might have noticed that this is one of the few beef recipes I've offered; the fact of the matter is that beef wasn't a huge item on the original Cracker table. Early Cracker cowmen were paid to *hunt* cows, not *eat* them. Corn Cracker dirt farmers raised more pigs than cows, as pork was easily salted and preserved and easier to butcher back in the day when it was just you and a knife.

But I am loath to insult the Modern Cracker Cattleman—a class of men who are polite to a fault, although they routinely carry pistols and have been known to hold a grudge. In the interest of making nice, I am presenting a dish made with a cut of beef that is on the cheap and tough side, which isn't a coincidence. When you think Cracker, think Cheap. Think $40 weekly grocery budget to feed a family of five. This simple recipe shines in the categories of taste, relatively healthy eating, and economy.

2 pounds beef sirloin tips
2 tablespoons canola oil
1 large yellow onion, thinly sliced
1 green bell pepper, seeded and
    thinly sliced
1 red bell pepper, seeded and
    thinly sliced
1 clove garlic, crushed through a
    garlic press
½ cup beef broth
One 14-ounce can stewed tomatoes
2 tablespoons soy sauce
Dash of hot sauce
Salt and ground black pepper to taste

1. Cut the sirloin tips into thin strips. Heat the oil in a cast-iron skillet over medium-high heat. Add the meat and sauté for 2 minutes, till browned.

2. Stir in the onion, peppers, garlic, broth, and tomatoes. Cook till tender, about 10 minutes if you want it more like stir-fry; cook it a little longer for true Southern mushiness.

3. Remove from the heat and season with soy sauce, hot sauce, salt, and pepper. Serve over prepackaged yellow rice, cooked according to the directions on the bag.

Serves 6

Broiled Cheesy Tomatoes

These are a snap to make and a welcome addition to any summer supper. Tomatoes and cheese are just one of those classic combinations that, as Daddy would say, you can't beat with a stick.

5 ripe large tomatoes
1 cup shredded Cheddar or Jack cheese
¼ cup freshly grated Parmesan cheese
½ cup mayonnaise
½ cup bottled Italian dressing
Salt and ground black pepper to taste

1. Preheat the broiler. Coat a cookie sheet with nonstick cooking spray.

2. Cut the tomatoes into ¼-inch slices and lay them out on the cookie sheet.

3. Combine the cheeses, mayonnaise, and Italian dressing in a small bowl and carefully mound 2 tablespoons of the cheese mixture in the center of each tomato slice.

4. Broil the tomatoes for about 5 minutes, till the cheese is bubbling and just beginning to turn brown.

5. Remove from the oven and sprinkle with salt and pepper.

Serves 5

Cornpone or Corn Muffins

Now cornpone is really just a variation on yer basic cornbread recipe, minus the eggs. If you really want it to look like pone, then cook it in the little corn-cob-shaped cast-iron bakers. If you don't have such a skillet, then you can make it in muffin tins; technically they'll still be cornpone, though they'll look like corn muffins.

1½ cups plain cornmeal
½ cup self-rising flour
1 teaspoon baking powder
Pinch of salt
1½ cups buttermilk
2 tablespoon bacon drippings or (for the
    health conscious) canola oil

1. Preheat the oven to 350°.

2. Combine the dry ingredients in a large bowl, then add the buttermilk and fat, just like for basic cornbread. Beat well.

3. Pour into either a greased cornpone baker or into a greased muffin pan (mini or regular size).

4. Bake until brown, 12 to 15 minutes for regular muffins or a little less for the pones. Most pone pans only make 10 or so at a time, so prepare yourself to make two or three batches (and careful with that pan for it will burn you).

Makes 1 dozen muffins

Homemade Brandied Peach Ice Cream

Homemade ice cream is a tried and true winner in the summer, and this brandied peach version is subtle and sublime. However, if you don't like peaches, you can customize the basic recipe with your own favorite fruit or candy or flavor. I've made English toffee ice cream, peanut butter cup ice cream, blueberry cheesecake—the variations are endless. Just make as directed, then add crushed candy or fruit. (Crushed is the operative word, because if you put it in whole, even small pieces will freeze to a gravel consistency and become too hard to eat.) If you're old-school Cracker and decide to do a Cracker Theme party, throw in a bag of chopped-up Goo-Goo Clusters. Make your guests guess what the flavor is. Whoever guesses correctly gets to take home the leftover cornpone.

2½ pounds fresh peaches, peeled, pitted, and finely chopped
½ cup sugar
1 pint half-and-half
One 14-ounce can sweetened condensed milk
2 tablespoons vanilla extract
1 tablespoon brandy flavoring
2 cups whole milk

1. Puree the peaches with the sugar and half-and-half in a blender.

2. Stir in the condensed milk, vanilla, and brandy. Pour into your ice-cream freezer bucket and add enough whole milk to fill to the fill line.

3. Follow the manufacturer's instructions to freeze the ice cream.

Serves 8

IV. FISH FRY

You might have gathered from the length of this menu that I am married to a fishing Cracker (as opposed to a hunting Cracker or a NASCAR Cracker)—one Wendel Ray Owens, proud son of Trumann, Arkansas (*land of the true man,* or so he told me thirty years ago on our first date).

On the next page is a picture of his sainted Granddad Hart (far right) posing with a mighty string of Mississippi River catfish, circa 1934.

Notice Granddad Hart's general lack of body fat, which was typical in Crackers before the advent of Kentucky Fried Chicken and Oreo Blizzards. He wore the overalls with authority, as he was a sharecropper by profession. Till the day he died, his

preferred method of reclining was to squat down on his haunches like a grasshopper, his weight on his heels, his butt an inch off the ground. He'd squat like that, smoking a cigarette or whittling a stick, for hours on end, with placid calm. He was a man who was seldom known to voice an angry word, and only then in his wife's defense.

Wendel didn't inherit his even temper but did get his loyalty and his kindness. Whenever he's caught in an unusual act of sweetness, I'll comment in a tone of sage wisdom, "Gits thet from his grandeddy," and everyone knows exactly what I mean, and that I am bestowing a great compliment.

He also inherited his granddad's love of fishing. After he moved to Florida and married me, Wendel was quickly absorbed by my own clan's fishing devotees, namely Daddy and Great-Uncle Gene, who owned a little fishing camp on the Apalachicola, way down in the woods, so isolated you could only get there by boat. It wasn't *by* the water but *on* the water—a couple of floating cabins linked by a floating catwalk. When the river was high, it was a little cabin floating in the middle of a very dark cypress swamp, which perfectly suited these lazy Crackers. As long as they didn't fall in the current (and become fish food in the gulf), they could run trotlines without stepping off the front porch.

Aunt Izzy called it The Ark. After she died, Uncle Gene, Daddy, and Wendel formed this Three Stooges–like fishing crew, and the fish-camp stories really never end.

The story that comes immediately to mind (and has nothing to do with fishing) is the time when Wendel was staying at the camp for an extended visit with Uncle Gene and Daddy. The camp didn't have running water, and after a couple of days, Daddy's breath got so bad that Wendel had to sleep at night with a sheet over his head. Since he was a mere son-in-law and Daddy a Cracker Patriarch, he couldn't find the words to tell him that his breath was so bad it was keeping him up nights.

Fortunately for Wendel, my brother Jeff stopped by to fish in the middle of the week. Being the kind of person who never minces words, Jeff told Daddy over coffee the next morning, "Daddy, I don't mean to insult you, but your breath could knock a buzzard off a shit wagon at fifty paces."

Daddy apologized and hastened to brush his teeth.

There is something to be said for honesty.

Well, I don't know how I got off on that. Oh, the fish camp, where frying fish isn't as de rigueur as it is at an actual fish fry but more commonly stewed. (Given that you're floating on a very dark river in the middle of some very dark woods and if you have a grease fire there, you're in for a very rough little swim.) Here's a mix-and-match menu. Don't feel any pressure to do it all in one fell swoop. Just pick and experiment and work out your own fish fry. Here's Daddy and Wendel with their own catfish, looking as proud as if they invented the creature, instead of just snagging it on a trotline.

Fried Catfish

I'll start with the old favorite, fried catfish. This recipe can be adjusted to fry grouper, redfish, and so on.

 1⅓ cups plain cornmeal
 ⅔ cups plain flour
 2 teaspoons seasoning salt
 1 teaspoon ground black pepper
 1 cup buttermilk
 1 teaspoon hot sauce
 1 pan-skinned and gutted catfish
   (about 4 pounds)
 Peanut oil for frying

1. Mix the cornmeal, flour, salt, and pepper in a large bowl.

2. In a different bowl, mix the buttermilk and hot sauce.

3. Rinse the catfish and pat dry. Dip in the buttermilk mixture, then coat with the cornmeal mixture.

4. Heat about 3 inches oil in a cast-iron Dutch oven over medium-high heat until hot but not smoking. Drop in the catfish and fry for about 4 minutes on each side. Don't crowd the fish or you'll end up with a soggy crust.

5. Take the catfish out of the oil with tongs and drain on a brown paper bag.

Serves 5

Mullet Spread

The humble mullet is close to the Cracker heart because they're easy to catch and you don't even have to bait your line. They're smoked and sold in plastic wrap at roadside stands around the South, and many Crackers get a hankering for them (my mother included).

Here's a spread that's good on Ritz Crackers. (I don't mean your rich relatives but the little ones made by Nabisco that you buy at the store.) It's a winner at poker nights and tailgate parties, too.

1½ pounds smoked mullet
2 teaspoons minced yellow onion
**   (dried is fine)**
2 teaspoons finely chopped celery
1 clove garlic, minced
2 tablespoons finely chopped dill pickle
1¼ cups mayonnaise
Small dash of Worcestershire sauce

1. Remove the skin from the mullet and pick out the thousand bones.
2. Combine all the ingredients in a large bowl and chill for at least 1 hour.
3. Serve as a spread for crackers, or as a dip for celery, or what have you.

Serves 8

Catfish Stew

Aside from his fish camp, Uncle Gene was famous for his extraordinary children and beautiful nieces, and last but not least, his catfish stew. I have his recipe somewhere, written in his own hand, but have by-gosh misplaced it. This is a reliable version from memory. It was traditionally made over a fish-camp fire and might be called the Cracker equivalent to Manhattan clam chowder. The recipe makes a powerful lot of stew and can be halved.

> **10 pounds filleted catfish**
> **4 pounds yellow onions, peeled and**
>   **chopped**
> **¾ cup catsup**
> **2 tablespoons hot sauce**
> **1 cup water**
> **10 pounds red potatoes, scrubbed and**
>   **chopped**
> **4 cups stewed tomatoes**
> **2 pounds bacon, cut into 2-inch strips,**
>   **roasted over a fire or fried in a pan**
> **Salt and ground black pepper to taste**

1. Put all the ingredients in a large pot and heat on the stove (or over a campfire) over medium heat for 1 hour or so, till the potatoes are tender.

2. Serve in bowls or just have everyone gather around with spoons. Elbows are allowed on the table.

Conch Chowder

Now conch chowder is one of those coastal Cracker things, and to tell you the truth, I'm not such a fan. For one thing, if you pick them up fresh and take them home and aren't careful about burying the shell, you're in for a big stinky house that will stay that way for days. This recipe begins with the assumption you can get yourself some shelled fresh conch (which, my friends, is a great big *snail*), and if you live in Key West or Cedar Key, you probably can. The end result is a pretty good seafood gumbo-like dish. It's always fun to inform your guests (especially if they're underlings or visiting in-laws) that they're eating a great big, cut-up *snail*.

1 pound conch meat
3 tablespoons strained Key lime juice
      (or regular lime juice if you don't
      grow Key limes)
¾ cup catsup
4 strips bacon, chopped
3 tablespoons olive oil
1 sweet onion, chopped
½ cup chopped celery
4 cloves garlic, minced
1 green bell pepper, seeded and
      chopped
4 tomatoes, seeded and chopped
1 pound white potatoes, peeled and
      diced
1 bay leaf
Hot sauce to taste
Salt and ground black pepper to taste

1. Cut the conch into nugget-sized pieces and place it in a medium bowl. Add the lime juice and catsup and toss to coat. Let marinate at least 1 hour.

2. Fry the bacon in a cast-iron skillet. Add the olive oil, onion, celery, garlic, and green pepper. Cook over medium-low heat until very lightly browned.

3. Add the tomatoes and simmer over medium heat for 5 minutes. Add the potatoes, marinated conch, and bay leaf. Cook over low heat for 1 hour or so.

4. Fish out the bay leaf and season with hot sauce, salt, and pepper to taste.

Serves 5

Peas Ambush

When my brother Jeff heard I was doing a cookbook, he hastened to call me with his own signature fish-camp favorite, which he feeds my nephews and their fishing buddies out on Island Lake when they gather there to fish, tell yarns, and eat curious man-food, like Peas Ambush. Add a can of mushroom soup, and it is transformed into another classic Cracker masterpiece: Trainwreck.

I suspect both recipes would be fitting side dishes to possum.

If I outlive Jeff, I plan to take them to his funeral party. When I stand to tell a story on him, it will almost definitely be about the week we moved to Ocala, when I was about eight and Jeff roughly ten. We were barefoot little scavengers, and to our great delight, the house's previous owners (or maybe it was the neighbors) had thrown away a bottle of cherry-red nail polish.

Well, Mama was Pentecostal and never wore nail polish, and we'd never seen such a thing in our lives. We were fascinated by the little brush and jewel color. Jeff took a great liking to it and not only painted my fingernails but also applied a coat to his own stubby nails, fingers and toes, both. To this day, I remember the incongruous sight of my crew-cut, snaggle-toothed brother, who was then (and always) a tough little fighter, going around in scruffy shorts and cherry-red nail polish, growing sullen and snappish when anyone questioned him on his choice of girly adornment.

I never understood it at the time, but looking back, I think, Oh, Jeffie! The anger, the repressed fundamentalism, the denial of his feminine side. Put it all together and it explains *so* much.

Incidentally, he now builds rocket engines for a living. He's the brother on the right here, striking a classic Cracker pose in front of Jay's new truck in 1978, when I still had big hair.

Jeff's recipe for Peas Ambush is nice for outdoor cooking because it is a one-dish meal. Jeff sometimes adds a little grated carrot during football season (he says) to give it go-Gator color. Make of that what you will.

1 package macaroni and cheese
One 3-ounce can tuna, drained
One 14-ounce can English peas, drained
¼ cup chopped yellow onion
1 cup coarsely chopped Cheddar cheese

1. Make the macaroni and cheese according to package directions in a medium saucepan.
2. Add the tuna, peas, onion, and cheese and simmer till the cheese is melted.

Serves 4, though my nephews have been
known to eat the whole pot between them,
which would be 2 servings

Roasted Oysters

Crackers really do believe the folklore about oysters and, well, *pleasure* might be the polite word. I personally think it accounts for their runaway popularity (I'm not too fond of them myself). I usually only eat them fried, but they're pretty good roasted (technically, steamed in their shells) if you work out the sliminess with a good fire.

But if you're using them as natural Viagra, well, hey, more power to you. Eat as many as you like. I'll be over in the corner eating orange pie.

3 dozen oysters in their shells
1 cup salt
Saltine crackers (the bread ones,
**   not your cousins)**
Melted sweet butter
Hot sauce

1. Wash the oysters well, scrubbing them with a brush if necessary. Fill a sink with water and mix in the salt. Add the oysters and let soak for 1 hour.

2. Heat a grill to medium heat; or dig a fire pit, make a fire in the ground, and cover it with a piece of tin, as old-school Crackers used to do. When the grill (or tin) is hot, put the oysters on and close the lid or cover with foil.

3. Cook briefly, only 5 minutes or so, till the oysters pop open.

4. Carefully remove them from heat (the shells will be hot) and pour them into a pile. Use your pocket knife to pry them open and eat on crackers with plenty of melted butter and hot sauce.

Serves 6

Beer Batter Fried Shrimp

Shrimp are to Crackers what crawdads are to Cajuns, which is to say: mighty fine. You can fry them in the same flour/cornmeal recipe I've given for fried catfish or do this tempura beer batter that is more along the lines of my aunt Doris's recipe, which she used to cook on Christmas Eve at her Grannie Party, when all her children and grandchildren would come over for their presents. It's an all-purpose beer batter and can be used to fry scallops (recipe follows) or whole mushrooms or onion rings.

Peanut oil for frying
2 large eggs, beaten
2 cups self-rising flour
1 teaspoon baking powder
1 tablespoon onion salt
One 12-ounce can beer
2 pounds shelled, deveined large shrimp
Salt to taste

1. Pour 3 inches of oil into a heavy cast-iron Dutch oven and heat over medium-high heat till oil bubbles around edge of pot.

2. Beat the eggs, flour, baking powder, onion salt, and beer in a large mixer bowl till smooth.

3. Dip the shrimp, a few at a time, in the batter and carefully drop them into the hot oil, with space left between them. Give the pot a little shake every so often to make sure they're not cooking in the same place. Fry about 3 minutes, till golden brown and bubbling.

4. Use a slotted metal spoon to dip them out of the hot oil and onto a brown paper bag to drain and dry. Spread so they're in one layer, still not touching, and sprinkle with salt to taste.

5. Keep frying till you're done, making sure your oil stays at a steady temperature.

Serves 4

Fried Scallops

Scallops are fun to harvest, like an aquatic Easter egg hunt. If you're interested, call down to the Big Bend area of North Florida, around Steinhatchee or Apalachicola, and you'll find plenty of boat-rental operations and directions on when the season exactly begins (roughly July through September). I prefer scalloping to fishing and hunting, as I get too hot sitting out in the sun fishing and am too deficient of attention to sit in a tree stand and wait for a deer to amble along. (Oh, yeah, and I'm scared of guns and don't like to see Bambi-like creatures slaughtered. That, too.)

Scalloping is a higher form of hunting; it's basically snorkeling with a purpose. While you're floating along, hunting for scallops tucked away in the sea grass, you get a first-hand view of all manner of wildlife: starfish, minnows, even a few sand sharks.

This recipe is Miss Katie B's favorite. Katie B (the B is for Obedience) is ninety-eight years old and might be said to be, truly, the Queen of the Crackers. (I'm only a Princess, you might recall.) She was my next-door neighbor for eleven years in Newberry and remains one of my role models for life. She is lovable, smart, chic, and civic minded, and, like all Cracker women of her generation, tough as a pine knot. Whenever we used to go scalloping, I'd come home, fry up a batch, and take her a plate while they were still hot.

> **Peanut oil for frying**
> **2 large eggs**
> **2 to 3 cups self-rising flour**
> **1 teaspoon baking powder**
> **1 tablespoon onion salt**
> **One 12-ounce can beer**
> **3 pounds shelled bay scallops**
> **Salt to taste**

1. Pour 2 inches of oil into a heavy cast-iron Dutch oven and heat over medium-high heat till oil bubbles around the edges of the pot.

2. Beat the eggs, flour, baking powder, onion salt, and beer in a large mixer bowl till smooth.

3. Dip the scallops, a few at a time, in the batter, and carefully drop them into the hot oil, with space left between them. Give the pot a little shake every so often to make sure they're not cooking in the same place. Fry for 1 to 2 minutes, till golden brown.

4. Use a slotted metal spoon to dip them out of the hot oil and onto a brown paper bag to drain and dry. Spread so they're in one layer, still not touching, and sprinkle with salt to taste.

5. Keep frying till you're done, making sure your oil stays at a steady temperature.

Serves 6

Hush Puppies

Hush puppies are the classic fish-fry favorite and really nothing but a spiced-up hoe-cake, dropped into grease instead of fried flat. The variations are endless. This is my tried-and-true old recipe with chopped onion, but you could add green onion, chopped jalapeño, or corn, or whatever you happen to have in your kitchen or garden the minute you start to mix them. I like sweet Vidalia onion, but use whatever little onion you find rolling around in your pantry, along with any other color, texture, or combo (Brie? Garlic? Thai?) that strikes your fancy.

2 cups white cornmeal
2 teaspoons baking soda
2 teaspoons salt
½ cup finely chopped Vidalia onion
1 large egg, beaten
1 cup buttermilk
4 to 5 tablespoons cold water
Peanut oil for frying

1. Mix the ingredients (except the oil) in the order listed, then add enough cold water to make it hold together. Shape into rounds or oblongs about as big as a walnut.

2. Heat 2 inches oil over high heat till it bubbles around the edges. Drop in the hush puppies, five or six at a time, and fry for 1 minute on each side, till they're nice and crunchy and uniformly brown. Like fried chicken, the secret to success with hush puppies is not to overload the fryer but to give every little hush puppy room to sizzle and cook without having to touch any of his brethren.

3. When they're brown, take them out with a slotted metal spoon and drain on a brown paper bag.

Serves 5

Aunt Izzy's Banana Pudding

No fish fry (or funeral) would be complete without a good old banana pudding. Here is Aunt Izzy's old-school recipe with custard filling and meringue topping, which can be served warm or cold. In really indulgent Cracker households, one was kept in the refrigerator for the cold devotees and one on the counter for the warm ones. My brother Jay was indulged in such a way as a child, which explains so much of his current temperament. I sometimes get a yen for brandy-flavored custard and add brandy along with the vanilla, and it is mighty fine. Delivers a little touch of bananas Foster.

This old-school version, made with canned milk—a favorite in the days before refrigeration—is easily transformed into a lazy Cracker favorite by replacing the meringue with whipped cream or whipped topping, and the custard with store-bought pudding (made according to package directions). But first give Aunt Izzy's old-school recipe a whirl. Like almost every other dessert in this book, it is even better the next morning, eaten with a glass of iced tea—I don't know why. I don't know the answer to all the mysteries of our Cracker world; I just enjoy them.

1 cup sugar, divided
⅓ cup self-rising flour
One 12-ounce can evaporated milk
3 large eggs, separated
2 tablespoons sweet butter, softened
1½ teaspoons real vanilla extract
3 cups vanilla wafers
3 bananas, peeled and sliced ¼ inch thick
½ teaspoon cream of tartar

1. Combine ¾ cup of the sugar, the flour, and milk in a heavy-bottomed saucepan and cook stirring over medium-low heat for 5 to 7 minutes, till thickened.

2. Beat the egg yolks in a small bowl, then stir about ½ cup of the hot mixture into them. Stir the egg yolk mixture into the remaining hot mixture, then stir in the butter and vanilla. Cook for another 3 minutes, until the mixture thickens again. Set aside and let cool.

3. Preheat the oven to 350°.

4. Line your favorite deep ovenproof dish (roughly 2 quarts) with vanilla wafers. Add a layer of sliced bananas, then pour on the pudding mixture.

5. Beat the egg whites in a large mixer bowl until foamy. Gradually beat in the remaining ¼ cup sugar and the cream of tartar. Beat on high for 3 minutes, till stiff. Spread this sweet meringue over the pudding.

6. Bake until the meringue is brown, not more than a minute or two. Keep an eye on it and have your oven gloves ready, as it browns quickly and many a lovely pudding has been ruined by a doggone burnt top.

Serves 8

Banana-Pineapple Pudding

Like every other Cracker classic, mutations do abound, and in this case, the mutation is nearly as tasty as the original. Since it is made with packaged pudding and doesn't have a meringue top, it's easier to make and really pretty ding-dang good.

One-half 16-ounce box gingersnaps
4 bananas, sliced
1 cup canned crushed pineapple, drained
Two 3.5-ounce packages instant vanilla pudding mix
2½ cups whole milk
One 16-ounce tub whipped topping, thawed
½ cup chopped pecans

1. Line a 9 x 13-inch inch pan with the cookies, then add a layer of banana, then pineapple (as if you were making a fruit lasagna).

2. Mix the dry pudding mix and milk with a hand mixer for 3 minutes, till smooth. Pour over the banana-pineapple mixture and chill for several hours or overnight.

3. Before serving, top with the whipped topping and sprinkle with pecans.

Serves 8

Here's a picture of domestic bliss at the table of a very civilized little fish fry. That's Uncle Dennis to the left, then Aunt Doris, Cousin Nelson, and Grannie, who is presiding over her end of the table with a face of beatific contentment (she did love to eat). They're having cole slaw and hush puppies with their fish, probably catfish or shellcracker (that is, sunfish) from Blue Run. Notice the beadboard wall to the rear, the willowware plates, green onions, and Sunday goblets, brimming with iced tea.

What you have here is Classic Cracker.

V. FROM YOUR SUMMER GARDEN

MENU

Butter Beans

Fresh Field Peas

Green Beans and New Potatoes

Fried Okra

Cucumbers in Sour Cream

Okra and Tomatoes

Hearts of Palm Salad

Red Potato Salad

Cold Potato Soup

Fried Cabbage

Modern Smashed Potatoes

Tomato, Onion, and Cucumber Marinade

Hoppin' John

For the vegetarian, the humane, and soft-hearted who are secretly appalled by the common Cracker's ability to digest anything that oinks, creeps, or crawls, here is a welcome relief from carnivorous cravings, straight from the summer garden. The list is long because Crackers were often without meat or even any convenient roadkill and made an art of the vegetable plate and cornbread dinner.

The beauty of this plate was that it could be grown at home in a tidy little truck garden, then canned for the rest of the year. The preserve jars were kept in plain sight in pie safes or on kitchen shelves as reassurance that we might be poor but we wouldn't starve. It was a symbol of plenty and any self-respecting Cracker woman was proud to show off her pie safe and pantry, filled with jarred green beans and tomatoes; peach butter and fig preserves. If she loved you, she'd give you some to take home.

Historically speaking, the most indigenous and rare of all Florida Cracker dishes is swamp cabbage, but since it kills the palmetto to harvest it, I will refrain from offering a recipe and begin with another old Southern scene stealer, the butter bean.

Butter Beans

Ah, the butter bean. Has there ever been a more modest, lusted-after little legume? A plate of butter beans, cornbread, and fried potatoes is a stock supper for Arkansas Crackers (believe me, I'm married to the Crown Prince). You can buy your beans frozen or canned, but here is the old-school way, seasoned with a touch of our friend, the ham. If you buy them outside the South, they're called "lima beans," but no worries. They're just the same.

1 pound shelled fresh butter beans
2 cups chicken broth
3 tablespoons sweet butter
1 small ham hock
1 tablespoon dried onion flakes
Pinch of sugar
1 teaspoon salt
1 teaspoon ground black pepper

1. Rinse the beans and put them in a medium pot with everything else.

2. Bring to a boil, then immediately turn down the heat and simmer uncovered for 1 hour or so, till the beans are tender. Aunt Izzy always mashed a few on the side of the pot to make it more creamy. A good rule of thumb is the longer you simmer, the creamier the beans. If you like them on the firm side, with a Yankee-like stiffness, then simmer for 30 minutes.

Serves 5

Fresh Field Peas

This humble dish has always been a family favorite among my mother's family—so mythic a little pea that my cousin Marcie once rejected a prospective suitor on the grounds that he passed on fresh field peas when offered them at the table. It just didn't set right with her, and now we call any vetting of suitors "the field pea test." Either you pass it or you don't, and there is no retest. Refusing to eat field peas for any reason is just a basic red flag. It speaks *volumes*.

4 cups fresh field peas
One 1-inch-thick slice salt pork
    (about 8 inches long), cut into
    2-inch pieces
1 small yellow onion, finely chopped
1 clove garlic, minced
1 teaspoon salt
1 teaspoon ground black pepper

1. Rinse the peas and put them in a large pot with enough water to cover.

2. Add the pork, onion, garlic, salt, and pepper. Cook uncovered over medium-low heat for 30 to 40 minutes, till the peas are tender. As with butter beans, you can mash a few against the side of the pot to make for a creamier, thicker dish.

Serves 8

Green Beans and New Potatoes

2 strips thick-sliced bacon

2 pounds fresh green beans, poles or climbers,
    ends snapped

1 small yellow onion, chopped

12 small red potatoes (about 1 inch in diameter),
    scrubbed

1 cup water

Salt and ground black pepper to taste

1. Put the bacon in a large pot and cook for 2 minutes over medium heat.

2. Add the beans, onion, potatoes, water, salt, and pepper.

3. Bring to a boil, then turn down the heat. Cover and simmer for 30 minutes, till the potatoes and beans are happily married and ready to eat.

Serves 8

Fried Okra

Like our Cajun cousins, we love okra (pronounced *oak-ree*) for its slimy deliciousness and for its economy. One okra bush will bear a thousand okra pods if you keep cutting them. They're good in gumbo and stew but are also good fried whole. If you are growing them, pick them when they're little and young, about 2 inches long. They get tougher the bigger they get, and an okra pod big enough to win first prize at the county fair won't be fit to feed the hogs. Where okra is concerned, size *does* matter.

1 pound small okra pods
⅔ cup coarsely ground cornmeal
1 teaspoon salt, plus more to taste
½ teaspoon ground black pepper,
     plus more to taste
1 large egg
1 cup peanut oil

1. Rinse the okra and trim the stems if needed.

2. Mix the cornmeal, salt, and pepper in a shallow bowl. Beat the egg in a second shallow bowl. Heat the oil in a cast-iron skillet over high heat till hot.

3. Dip the okra first in the egg, then coat with the cornmeal mixture and carefully drop into the hot oil a few pods at a time, careful not to crowd. Fry for about 3 minutes, till golden brown.

4. Drain on a brown paper bag and sprinkle with salt and pepper while still hot.

Serves 5

Cucumbers in Sour Cream

Like okra, cucumbers grow in abundance all over Cracker Florida. Pair them with sour cream and you have a mild and modest little pleaser, a sure hit when you need a cold salad that is simple to make.

2 large cucumbers
2 cups boiling water
½ cup sour cream
2 teaspoons sugar
1 teaspoon finely chopped fresh chives
1 teaspoon chopped fresh dill
1 teaspoon salt
Dash of freshly ground black pepper

1. Peel and slice the cucumbers very thin.

2. Put the cucumber slices in a bowl and cover with the boiling water. Let stand for 5 minutes, then drain and rinse with cold water.

3. Mix the sour cream, sugar, chives, dill, salt, and pepper in a medium bowl. Toss in the cucumbers and mix well.

4. Chill before serving.

Serves 4 or 5

Okra and Tomatoes

A rare healthy Cracker dish that really is good. It can be served on rice or as a side dish.

2 tablespoons sweet butter
1 large sweet onion, chopped
1 pound whole okra (little ones)
One 10-ounce can stewed tomatoes
1 teaspoon salt
½ teaspoon ground black pepper

1. Melt the butter in a medium saucepan over medium heat, then toss in everything else.

2. Cook uncovered for 20 minutes, till everything is as limp as a dishrag, stirring occasionally.

Serves 5

Hearts of Palm Salad

This is another true Cracker original, or so they say in restaurants that serve it. I myself never ate such a salad till I moved to Gainesville to attend UF, but far be it from me to insinuate that someone just made it up. If you were raised on it, take no offense. Since hearts of palm here are commercially grown, I have no guilt in including it in a dish.

⅓ cup salad oil
2 tablespoons fresh lemon juice
1 teaspoon sugar
½ teaspoon salt
2 tablespoons chopped green olives
1 tablespoon finely chopped
    yellow onion
1 tablespoon finely chopped celery
One 14-ounce can hearts of palm,
    drained and sliced
6 cups torn Bibb lettuce
1 cup vinaigrette dressing

1. Combine the salad oil, lemon juice, sugar, salt, olives, onion, and celery in a medium bowl and chill for at least 1 hour.

2. Just before serving, toss with the hearts of palm and lettuce in a large salad bowl. Add the vinaigrette and toss again.

Serves 6

Notes on Poke Salad

Traditionally speaking, there is no salad more Cracker than poke salad. On a lean day, you'd just go out with a shotgun full of birdshot and shoot you up some blackbirds, then pick a handful of poke salad. Alas, it has now been revealed as toxic (the weed, not the bird). Eat it and it'll kill you, or at least that's what they say these days. Why it never killed our grandmothers, I do not know. Maybe it has something to do with women's liberation. Just beware.

It is apparently not as innocent a little weed as it seems.

Red Potato Salad

I love red potatoes because they are nutritious, tasty, and you don't have to peel them. They are God's gift to lazy cooks everywhere. Some people prefer their potato salad with sweet pickles, but I'm a straight dill woman. Whenever I inadvertently bite into a deviled egg or potato salad with sweet pickles, I make a pained and ugly face.

This is served warm or cold and is especially good with country ham.

4 medium red potatoes
2 large eggs
1 medium yellow onion, chopped
½ cup mayonnaise
¼ cup horseradish sauce
½ cup chopped dill pickles
1 teaspoon paprika
1 teaspoon salt
½ teaspoon ground black pepper

1. Scrub the potatoes and slice ¼ inch thick. Put them in a large pot and add enough water to cover. Bring the water to boil. Add the eggs, cover the pot, and turn the heat down to medium-high. Cook for 10 minutes, till the potatoes are just tender.

2. Drain and let cool. Put the potatoes in a large bowl.

3. Peel and chop the eggs. Add the eggs, onion, mayonnaise, horseradish sauce, pickles, paprika, salt, and pepper to the potatoes. Toss gently to combine.

Serves 4

Cold Potato Soup

Depending upon your station in life, you'll call this dish either vichyssoise (that is, *vishy-swahz*) or cold tater soup. If you are a Metro Cracker and prefer the former, don't worry if you sound like Deputy Dawg speaking French, because that's how Cajuns sound, and they're the real deal.

4 cups peeled and chopped white potatoes
1 medium Vidalia onion, finely chopped
2 quarts chicken broth or homemade stock
1 teaspoon ground sea salt
½ cup heavy cream
1 teaspoon coarsely ground black pepper
2 tablespoons thinly sliced fresh chives or green onion

1. Put the potatoes, onion, broth, and salt in a large saucepan and simmer uncovered for 40 to 50 minutes.

2. Take off the heat and mash the potatoes till smooth with a potato masher. Add the cream and pepper and blend well.

3. Chill till cold. Before serving, garnish with the chives.

Serves 8

Fried Cabbage

There isn't a dish in this book easier to construct or more guaranteed to garner comments and requests for the recipe as this one. The addition of hot sauce is optional, but delicious, and gives it a slightly pink tint. If you're really up against the wall about what to bring to that special Valentine's Day dinner, this might be the dish. If you leave out the bacon, you'll have a truly nutritious low-cal dish. My problem is that I can't bring myself to leave out the bacon.

    4 ounces thick-sliced bacon
    1 large yellow onion, chopped
    1 large head green cabbage, shredded
    ½ cup water
    1 teaspoon salt
    1 teaspoon ground black pepper
    1 tablespoon hot sauce

1. Fry the bacon in a cast-iron Dutch oven over medium-high heat, till crisp. Drain, then break it up into crumbles.

2. Toss the onion into the bacon fat. Sauté over medium-high heat for 1 minute. Add the cabbage, water, salt, and pepper and cover the pan. Cook over low heat for 30 to 40 minutes, till it's wilted. It should be the consistency of cooked collards.

3. Add the hot sauce and toss well.

Serves 8

Modern Smashed Potatoes

I like this recipe for two reasons: It's delicious and easy, and like my red potato salad, it doesn't require peeling a big old mountain of potatoes. It is lumpier and more colorful than smooth mashed potatoes and has more fiber, I expect. Any gravy in this book (except chocolate) works well with this or even with just a little melted butter on top. You can throw in a few chopped chives for color or more paprika if you're a big paprika fan.

9 or 10 small red potatoes, scrubbed
½ cup sour cream
1 teaspoon seasoning salt
½ teaspoon ground black pepper
¼ cup salted butter

1. Put the potatoes in a medium pot, cover with water, and boil uncovered for 20 minutes.

2. Pour off the water, add the remaining ingredients, and smash it all up with a potato masher or fork till it's smoothly lumpy.

Serves 4

Tomato, Onion, and Cucumber Marinade

No Cracker cookbook is complete without a mention of this wonderful medley of flavor that in the early years of Cracker economy went right from the garden to the refrigerator to the table with no detours at the oven, which was a blessing before the advent of air conditioning. Purists eat it without anything but salt and pepper, but I'm adding vinaigrette for a swankier effect, and an opportunity to speak French again, if you're looking to impress.

4 ripe tomatoes
3 fresh cucumbers, peeled
1 sweet Vidalia onion, peeled
1 cup sugar
¾ cup white vinegar
½ cup vegetable oil
½ teaspoon salt
1 teaspoon ground black pepper

1. Cut the tomatoes, cucumbers, and onion into ¼-inch-thick slices and combine in a large bowl. Put aside in the refrigerator while you make your vinaigrette.

2. Combine the sugar, vinegar, oil, salt, and pepper salt in a small saucepan and bring to boil. Stir and remove from the heat. Let cool to room temperature.

3. Pour the marinade on the vegetables, toss to combine, and refrigerate for at least 1 hour, till well chilled.

Serves 6

Hoppin' John

As the saying goes: Peas and rice; they're always nice.

½ **cup dried black-eyed peas**
4 cups water
½ **teaspoon red pepper flakes**
1 tablespoon minced garlic
One 8-ounce ham hock
¼ **cup uncooked rice**
½ **cup chopped yellow onion**
½ **cup chopped green bell pepper**
1 teaspoon salt
½ **teaspoon ground black pepper**

1. Put the peas and water in a large Dutch oven and heat to boiling. Boil for a couple of minutes, then cover and let stand for 1 hour.

2. Stir in the red pepper flakes, garlic, and ham and simmer uncovered for 1 hour.

3. Stir in the rice, onion, bell pepper, salt, and pepper. Cover and simmer for 30 minutes, till the peas are tender and the rice is done.

Serves 6

All Manner of Unclean Beast, Football, and One Little Bitty Baby, Born in Bethlehem

Autumn is the kindest season of all in Cracker Florida, with the brutal sun turned to a milder angle, burned down from the summer's blistering white heat. Autumn in Cracker Country offers the best of both worlds: a prolonged Indian summer that stretches from Labor Day till Christmas and not much in the way of frost. Historically, it was the season of peanut harvest, hay cutting, cane grinding, and spooky, prank-filled Halloweens. Rural Crackers still abide by these farming traditions, at least peripherally, but even out here in the country, autumn is now ruled by the academic calendar: back-to-school sales, homeroom assignments, PTA Fall Festivals, and the massive rattle of big old yellow school buses churning up the dust on our dirt road.

Crackers were never great supporters of federal education, until the wily Yanks created a sure-fire method of instilling loyalty to the local high school by attaching them to the great Southern religion that is football. Gone are the days when strapping big boys were hidden by their grandpas in the corn crib so they wouldn't be picked up by truant officers and brainwashed by public education. They're now star linebackers who take to the field every Friday night in epic pigskin battles that are fought tooth and nail by hometown teams with ferocious names: Bobcats, Wildcats—or in one startling example of intimidation: the Big Green Indians (of Choctawhatchee High School, Ft. Walton, Florida).

A whole little universe of ceremony and tradition have sprung up around these games: homecoming, tailgating, boiled peanuts, and Booster Fundraising barbecues, to name but a few, that stretch well into November. That's when yet another dearly loved Cracker obsession takes its place: hunting, in all its intricate variations: bow season, then black powder, then, finally, finally, that most exalted of all weeks in the hunter's calendar: deer season.

I. WILD GAME DAYS/HUNTING SEASON

Here is the thing with Crackers: They like the great outdoors, they like weaponry, and they take literally the scriptural imperative to take dominion over the beasts of the field. Bring all these elements together, and what you get is the picture, on the next page, of Jay striking a classic Cracker pose with a dead deer about to be butchered. Some hunters would grin at this point, but Jay has a look of serious modesty at bagging what looks to be a seven-point buck (count the tips on the antlers). His camo-overalls are a good example of the benefits of a fusion culture (farming + hunting = cool new clothes).

If you think eating wild game a little ghoulish, then brace yourself for even stranger provender to come, as Crackers were human scavengers for a good part of their evolutionary process and there are few species they haven't baked, spitted, or boiled.

Our official Florida Cracker expert, my buddy Dana Ste. Clair, swears that when he was a boy growing up around Scrambletown, Crackers in the Ocala National Forest wouldn't let roadkill stay on Highway 40 for long, but would swiftly shovel it in their trunks and take it home for supper. I don't doubt his word but must add that even when Daddy was making $20 a week selling burial policies in Mississippi, I never remember having to eat anything that had actually been scraped off the asphalt.

But, hey, it does use the resource. So if you happen to hit a deer or a possum or an armadillo (who get hit so often because they're nearsighted and wander up on the road), just jump out and bag that baby. Then run home and by-gosh figure out how to dress it (cut off the head, gut, skin, or de-armor). Give it a little soak in soda (because all wild game really should be soaked to remove the gaminess). Then use one of the recipes here and cook you up a Venison Roast, or better yet, a mess of Possum and Sweet Potatoes, and serve it to your guests at a tailgate party. If they're Georgia fans, they'll eat it quick, then ask, "Since when do you eat possum with sweet potatoes? We always eat it with mashed potatoes." Georgia Crackers are just like that, sometimes, so eternally *superior*, ever since *Gone With the Wind.*

Venison Roast

It is hard to explain the cultural energy given to the pursuit of the deer in the rural Cracker South. Go into any rural Wal-Mart, from Homosassa to Hiawassee, year round, and you'll find eleven aisles of merchandise devoted solely to hunting: bows, ammo, and camo, not to mention deer pee, mosquito repellent, and expert manuals on everything from skinning to state regulations (there are a few these days).

Since Wendel is more a fisherman than a hunter, I only get venison when Burger has mercy on me and gives me some her husband has shot. I'd like to say she gives me the back strap (prime cut) but usually it's ground venison mixed with pork fat that can be cooked like ground beef. You add the fat to make it easier to cook because venison is naturally lean. (Ever seen a fat deer?)

If you're married to a hunter or have very generous friends and come upon a real venison roast, this recipe is as lean and tasty as an eye of round. The only catch is that if the actual hunter who killed it is at the table, your dining experience will be slightly dampened by his inevitable and interminable bragging on his superior skill in the hunt, and how tender it is, and how deer are really overpopulated, and it is a mercy to kill them before they starve—and so on and so forth.

After supper he'll want to take you out and show you his new four-wheeler. Consider yourself forewarned.

> **One 2- to 3-pound venison roast (Try not to run it
>   to death before you kill it, or all the soaking
>   in the world won't help. Use that $200 rifle sight
>   and get it clean on the first shot.)**
> **Buttermilk for soaking**
> **5 cloves garlic, peeled**
> **1 cup water**
> **1 teaspoon seasoning salt**
> **1 teaspoon ground black pepper**

1. Rinse your roast well, then put it in a large bowl and soak it in buttermilk overnight to remove the gaminess.

2. When you're ready to cook, preheat the oven to 325°.

3. Pour off the buttermilk and put the roast in a cast-iron Dutch oven. Stab it a few times with a knife and insert the cloves of garlic. Add the water to the pan and season the roast with salt and pepper.

4. Cover and bake for 1½ hours.

Serves 5

Fried Rabbit

We have a few rabbit families living out in our woods—wild brown bunnies who dart to the front of the woods and stand on their hind legs, noses twitching, and watch me pass when I go for a walk in the afternoon. I really can't see why anyone would feel the need to shoot and eat one unless they're starving. In that case, eat away. If not, well, Hardee's is open late these days. Go git you a chicken sandwich. Leave them bunnies alone.

But if you must, here's how.

> **4 cups water**
> **¼ cup regular salt**
> **1 skinned rabbit (already dressed, because I**
>   **really don't feel up to walking you through**
>   **the dismemberment of such an adorable**
>   **species), cut into serving pieces**
> **1 cup self-rising flour**
> **1 teaspoon seasoning salt**
> **1 teaspoon ground black pepper**
> **2 large eggs**
> **Peanut oil for frying**

1. Mix the water and regular salt in a large pot, add the rabbit, and boil for 30 minutes.

2. While it's boiling, mix the flour, seasoning salt, and pepper in a large bowl. Beat the eggs in another bowl.

3. When the rabbit has finished boiling, pour off the salt water and pat the rabbit pieces dry. Dip each piece first in the beaten eggs, then well with the flour mixture.

4. Put 3 inches of oil in a heavy-bottomed pot and heat till hot and bubbling around the edges.

5. Drop in the rabbit pieces and fry till golden brown, about 3 minutes on each side.

Serves 2 or 3

Fried Cooter (and this is possibly not what you think it is, if you're snickering)

The Cross Creek crowd is crazy about this small delicacy, which is basically fried turtle (NOT gopher). I mean fried little-turtle-on-the-log, freshwater turtle—the ones you see when you're canoeing down the Ocklawaha, sunning on a rock with their wives and children, with not a clue that you're eyeing them for the pot.

If you get them during molting season when their shells are soft, you have soft-shell turtle. Either way, it's basically eating a little green turtle, probably the kindly uncle of the little pet turtle you used to keep in an aquarium when you were a child.

Eat if you must.

Oh, and by the way, the word *cooter* has another, less aquatic meaning in the Cracker South. If you tell a real Cracker you had cooter for supper the night before, don't be surprised if you get a snicker (and possibly a congratulatory wink). When my daughters were little giggling girls, Emily found a recipe for cooter stew in some high-end Southern cooking magazine and couldn't handle it. She gathered her sisters and read it to them, and they literally fell out, all of them, crawling around on the carpet till they got the better of their laughter and could act like they had good sense.

1 freshwater turtle, at least 10 inches in diameter,
    about 2 pounds
½ cup white vinegar
1½ cups plain flour
1 teaspoon seasoning salt
1 teaspoon ground black pepper
One 12-ounce can evaporated milk
Peanut oil for frying

1. De-shell the turtle and scrape off the skin. Cut off the legs, neck, and tail (and bury them deep in the backyard, or your dogs will dig it back up and have a stinky turtle feast of their own).

2. Cut the turtle meat into bite-sized pieces and put it in a medium saucepan. Add the vinegar and enough water to cover and simmer covered for about 1 hour (to tenderize; cooters hold a grudge and don't go easily into that dark night).

3. Drain the meat and rinse.

4. Mix the flour, salt, and pepper in a medium bowl. Put the evaporated milk in a separate bowl.

5. Dip the meat pieces first in the milk, then roll in the flour mixture.

6. Heat 2 inches of peanut oil in a heavy-bottomed pot and fry till golden brown, about 3 minutes, in small batches, careful not to crowd.

Serves 4

Fried Frog Legs

Frog gigging is a cross between hunting and fishing and is especially popular on the Mississippi Delta, where Wendel was born. He was invited to go gigging one night when we were visiting years ago, to carry the pistol, they said. I couldn't understand how a pistol came into gigging frogs, and he explained that the water moccasins were so aggressive up there that they would actively pursue you—slither into your boat or fall on you from overhanging trees, sometimes two at a time—hence the necessity of bringing along a shooter with a pistol.

The story made a shocking impression on me and explains why we've never been real big frog-leg eaters around here. I say if a snake is that protective of his habitat and his frog friends (his dinner companions, I imagine, on many a hungry night), then let him have it.

> **12 pairs frog legs, skinned and ready to cook,**
> **with flappers removed (unless you can't**
> **live without them)**
> **1 cup buttermilk**
> **1 cup self-rising flour**
> **1 teaspoon seasoning salt**
> **1 teaspoon ground black pepper**
> **Peanut oil for frying**

1. Put the frog legs in a large bowl and and enough buttermilk to cover. Soak for at least 1 hour.

2. In a separate bowl, mix the flour, salt, and pepper

3. Drain the frog legs and coat with the flour mixture.

4. Heat 2 inches of peanut oil in a cast-iron Dutch oven over medium-high heat. Drop in the frog legs, no crowding. Fry for about 2 minutes, then flip them to the other side and fry for another 2, till brown.

Serves 4 or 5

Baked Armadillo

Yes, the little armored creature you so often see dead on the shoulder of southern highways is actually edible. Like pork, it is often eaten with rice or slathered in barbecue sauce. (Then you have Barbecued Armadillo, and if you're looking to win a prize as Crackerest Cook on Earth, that recipe might do the trick.) I personally think armadillos are so attractive that I really couldn't find the words to tell you how to butcher one. I will begin with the assumption that you have some armadillo meat on hand. To barbecue, just dab on your favorite sauce in the last 10 minutes of baking.

One 2-pound armadillo roast
½ cup sweet butter, melted
1 teaspoon onion salt
1 teaspoon ground black pepper
Red pepper flakes to taste

1. Preheat the oven to 325°.

2. Put the little beast in a roasting pan. Pour the melted butter over it, then sprinkle with the onion salt, pepper, and red pepper flakes.

3. Cover and bake for 30 minutes. Take off the lid and bake for another 15 minutes (for a crispier creature).

Serves 4

Rattlesnake

Now here is a Cracker specialty that will give you a run for your money. Unlike the kindly little river turtle or the puff-tailed bunny, this one bites back, and if he beats you to the draw, he'll send you straight to heaven or for a visit with my friend Sue on the medical intensive care unit at Shands-UF. I'm suggesting commercial rattlesnake meat as a start, so no one will spot a local rattler in their yard and decide to go after it with a garden hoe. Believe me when I say that the snake will win and end up frying *you*. And humans are so hard to skin.

For real rattlesnake-meat lovers, read Harry Crews's modern Cracker classic *A Feast of Snakes*. The last scene will give fair warning of what happens when you get too attached to your local rattlers.

2 pounds commercial rattlesnake meat
1 large egg, beaten
1 cup buttermilk
1 cup plain flour
1 teaspoon garlic salt
Peanut oil for frying

1. Rinse the rattlesnake meat and cut into nugget-sized pieces.

2. Beat the egg and buttermilk in one bowl and mix up the dry ingredients in another. In that same old Cracker frying refrain, dip the meat in the egg mixture, then in the flour mixture.

3. Heat 3 inches of oil in a cast-iron Dutch oven over high heat. Add the meat in batches to the oil and fry until golden brown, about 3 minutes on each side.

Serves 4, or up to 8 if served as an appetizer

Roast Possum and Sweet Potatoes

These curious little creatures are frequently portrayed as adorable and harmless and are even hand raised as pets, but let me tell you, they're about as mean as a rattlesnake in the wild. They're not aggressive, but they have these little poked-out teeth and know how to use them when provoked. True, they will faint (go sull) on you if they're sufficiently frightened (and they're not faking it—they really do faint), but I've known of a few hounds taking a licking off a possum, so be forewarned.

They're also in that particularly unclean class of Cracker delicacies (along with crabs and catfish) known as the scavenger class. If you don't know what that means, let me paint you a picture. My hunter friend Wayne once came upon a rotting dead cow, and for some reason (he was a kid; maybe curiosity) he gave it a thump, then let out a scream because three angry little possums emerged. They were eating the cow from the inside out. When you eat possum, you eat what he has already eaten, putting yourself at a fairly low notch on the food chain.

But what the hey. Some people love roast possum and sweet potatoes. I myself don't eat them, but I don't look down my nose at those who do. If you're having me over for supper and cooking possum, give me a little heads-up, and I'll drop by Hardee's for that chicken sandwich on my way.

1 cleaned possum
4 cups water
½ cup salt
¼ cup bacon drippings
Ground black pepper to taste
1 tablespoon brown sugar (like you'd
    put on a country ham)
4 peeled and halved sweet potatoes

1. Dress out your possum. (By which I mean kill, skin, and gut it. Put out of your mind the cool idea of serving it head-on, as the French sometimes serve duck.

Go ahead and remove the dang head and tail. If you don't do it for yourself, do it for me.)

2. In a large bowl, mix the water and salt. Soak the possum in it for at least 1 hour.

3. Preheat the oven to 350°.

4. Pour off the brine and rinse the meat. Add the bacon drippings, then the meat to a roasting pan and sprinkle with pepper and the brown sugar and any other favorite seasonings (garlic, rosemary—anything that works with pork).

5. Surround with the sweet potatoes. Roast covered for 1½ hours, until it looks brown and tasty.

Serves 4

Stewed Squirrel

This is another of Aunt Doris's famous dishes, as Uncle Dennis liked to hunt squirrels and both of them liked to eat. Daddy grew up eating squirrel and took much flak in the army for admitting to it. He claims northern soldiers considered squirrels rats with bushy tails, which, now that I think of it, isn't such a far-fetched description. In any case, squirrels have always been plentiful in the Cracker landscape and for many years served as the equivalent of wild-game, fast-food takeout.

**2 tablespoons salted butter or
  bacon drippings
1 yellow onion, chopped
¼ cup plain flour
2 squirrels, skinned, gutted, and cut
  into serving pieces
2 cups beef broth
½ teaspoon salt
½ teaspoon ground black pepper
1 cup whole milk**

1. Melt the butter in a large cast-iron Dutch oven over medium heat. Add the onion and cook for 2 minutes.
2. Add the flour and cook, stirring for another minute. Add the squirrels, broth, salt, pepper, and last of all, the milk.
3. Cook covered over low heat for 45 minutes, adding more milk if necessary.
4. Serve over rice.

Serves 2 to 4

Notes on Gopher Turtles

Like many Alabama pioneers, my great-great-grandmother Canadasier Troxell Jackson was part Native American, making her about as tribal an old Cracker as you'd ever want to meet. She was a granddaughter of George Jacob Troxell, the son of a Jewish trader who married among the Cherokee and became one of the last of the Kentucky longhunters, making me roughly one-thousandth Jewish. I bring this bit of historical minutia to your attention because that small (but vocal) strand in the helix of my DNA is getting really disgusted with this section on unclean beasts.

So I'll close it up on possum, though I do want to take the pulpit for a brief sermon in defense of a native creature that is being pushed out of his scrubby woods at an alarming speed and might someday be extinct: the lowly gopher turtle. When that happens, I'll move to Boston and call myself a Yankee because the South won't be worth inhabiting anymore. Furthermore, I'll be too ashamed to call myself a Cracker because we were poor stewards of the land and let civilization extinguish this sweet-natured little beast of the field who has always been good to us and kept many a Cracker alive in times of drought and want, and if that weren't enough, dug the tunnels that helped aerate our fields.

Back then, the gopher turtle was eaten out of economic necessity and variously referred to as Cracker Chicken or (by my father) as Hoover Hog. But those days are long past. I must insist that it is time that we return the favor and give our old friend refuge in our yards and fields. I live on twenty pristine West Alachua County acres and have given my back ten acres to a whole gopher turtle village. They are so shy I never see them, but I know they're alive and kicking because they have a dozen holes out there and little claw marks where they dig in or expand their households.

The old prejudice against gopher turtles was that rattlesnakes cohabit with them in their holes—which is true enough. I have a sure-fire remedy for not getting bit: Stay the hell away from their holes. If you happen across a rattler and it's you or him (or more likely, him or one of your yipping dogs), then kill him and eat him. Word will get back to the rest of the snakes and they won't bother you again. You'll be known as a snake eater. But let the turtle go. He can't help it if he's fond of the earth and likes to dig. Hell, if you were a lonely old turtle, you'd probably invite a snake or two in for the night. I say, live and let live.

And if you come across one dangerously close to the highway, safely stop, get out, pick him up on both sides of his shell, walk him to a safe place, and put him down in the same direction he was going (the other side of the street, if that's where he was heading). The exception to this rule is our vast and annoying interstate system. I think it's illegal to save the wildlife there. But you're free to save gopher turtles and even the occasional nonpoisonous snake on the back roads, and while you're taking them to safety, you might take the opportunity to warn them of the dangers of highway travel when you're only four inches tall. Apparently the word hasn't gotten out. And don't you dare intentionally run over a gopher turtle, and then take it home under the roadkill rule. You'll know it's a lie and so will your Maker.

II. TAILGATE PARTY

MENU

Red Beans and Rice

Dilled Shrimp

Broccoli and Raisin Salad

Asian Cole Slaw

Mississippi Mud Cake

Only slightly less celebrated than deer hunting and eating roadkill is the Cracker's love of football and the curious custom of turning home games into holy communions, where like-minded fans gather to ruminate, pray for a winning season, and eat like there is no tomorrow. Wendel's day job is as a production superintendent with Anheuser Busch, and every year we host a Bull Gator tailgate that has gotten to be an increasingly elaborate event, with much anticipation when our turn to host comes around. A couple years ago a maintenance guy at the plant came with his two sons, both of whom (I think) are bachelors. After a generous sampling of our table and company product, they grew misty-eyed and sentimental.

When the father left, he shook Wendel's hand and thanked him sincerely (and repeatedly) for setting such a fine table and wouldn't let go. It was a full 60-second Cracker lovefest of gratitude and flattery, till he finally just drew him into a tearful clutch and muttered, "I love you, man."

That's what the correct combination of football and beer can do to a man—reduce him to tears.

Red Beans and Rice

I don't know how they do it up in Athens or Tuscaloosa or Columbia, but here in Gator Nation, we have three essential components to the Classic Tailgate. One is seafood, the other barbecue (usually pulled pork from a local place) and the last is some sort of savory, spicy stew, such as this dish of Red Beans and Rice I started making a couple of years ago. It was such a hit that I'm now its prisoner and have to bring it every year.

This is a Louisiana dish, and like all Louisiana dishes, the variations are endless. Use this as your founding recipe and tweak to your heart's content. You can serve this over rice at home (and much more gravy than rice), but if you're making it for a tailgate, just cook up a cup of rice and add it in. My friend from New Orleans assures me that the ratio of gravy to rice must be three to one, or you're not really eating red beans and rice.

> **1 pound dried red kidney beans**
> **¼ cup salted butter**
> **1 large yellow onion, chopped**
> **1 green bell pepper, chopped**
> **5 ribs celery, chopped**
> **3 cloves garlic, minced**
> **2 small ham hocks**
> **1 to 1½ pounds mild or hot smoked**
>   **sausage links**
> **½ teaspoon dried thyme leaves**
> **1 bay leaf**
> **Dash of Worcestershire sauce**
> **Pinch of red pepper flakes**
> **½ teaspoon hot sauce**

1. Put the beans in a large pot and add water to cover. Soak overnight (or use the quick-boil method on the bag). When you're ready to cook, pour off the water and cover with fresh water. Bring to a high simmer over medium-high heat and cook for about 1 hour.

2. While the beans are cooking, melt the butter in a cast-iron skillet over medium-high heat. Add the onion, bell pepper, celery, and garlic and sauté for about 5 minutes.

3. Add the vegetables, ham hocks, sausage, and seasonings to the simmering beans and bring to a boil. Reduce the heat, cover, and simmer for 2 hours. Stir often in the last hour to make sure the beans don't stick. If your liquid is boiling out too fast, add 1 more cup water.

4. Serve over long-grained rice, made according to package directions.

Serves 8

Dilled Shrimp

My thieving husband, Wendel, purloined a recipe from Pat Conroy's cookbook for bar-becued shrimp, which he claims as his own. I haven't stooped to thievery (yet), and we usually bring two shrimp dishes to the game—his stolen one and my authentic one, and a cooler, happier little shrimp dish you couldn't ask for.

1½ cups mayonnaise
1 cup sour cream
Juice of 1 lemon
⅓ cup sugar
1 big red onion, thinly sliced
2 tablespoons dried dill or, even better,
    chopped fresh dill
3 pounds medium shrimp, peeled, deveined,
    and boiled till just pink

1. Mix everything but the shrimp in a large sealable plastic bowl. Toss in the shrimp and stir till well mixed.
2. Seal and let marinate in the refrigerator overnight. Give the bowl a shake occasionally to make sure everything is marinating evenly.
3. Serve chilled.

Serves 6

Broccoli and Raisin Salad

I make this tangy little salad every year for tailgating parties, but it is also great for fish fries with its salty, crunchy, sweet, and chewy texture. It's another recipe that people fall in love with and nag you to make every year. "You know, thet raisin and peanut thang—with the broccoli 'n all."

2 cups raw broccoli florets
½ cup chopped yellow onion
½ cup raisins
½ cup Spanish peanuts
1 cup mayonnaise
½ cup sugar
2 teaspoons white vinegar

In a large sealable plastic bowl, mix all the ingredients together. Chill for at least 2 hours, but preferably overnight.

Serves 4 and can be doubled
(or tripled if you're feeding our football crew)

Asian Cole Slaw

When you get to the pig-picken section, you might wonder if there is any end to my cole slaws, and the answer is no. Here is another big hit at the tailgate, and it's easy to make. It's also good at fish fries, pig-pickens, and NASCAR cookouts. It doesn't have mayo, so you don't have to worry about killing off your kinsmen with food poisoning if it's going to sit out all day in the sun.

> **2 packages chicken-flavored ramen noodles,**
> **broken into pieces**
> **One 16-ounce package shredded cole slaw mix**
> **½ cup sliced almonds, toasted**
> **1 bunch green onions, chopped**

While the noodles are still in the package, crush them into pieces. In a large bowl, mix them with the cole slaw mix, almonds, and green onions.

DRESSING

> **½ cup sugar**
> **¾ cup canola oil**
> **⅓ cup white vinegar**
> **2 seasoning packets from the ramen noodles**

Mix the sugar, oil, vinegar, and seasoning from the noodles together in a small bowl till well blended. At least 1 hour before serving, pour the dressing over the slaw mix and toss well. Chill till you're ready to leave for the game.

Serves 5

Mississippi Mud Cake

Mud cake is another old Gatorland favorite, beloved for its cold and crunchy variety of texture: gooey, chocolate, and wonderful. But let me give you fair warning about Mississippi Mud Cake: It's as rich as Midas and will make you sick if you eat too much of it. I was once felled by such an illness at a funeral when I was a kid. One piece is divine; two pieces might be lethal.

1 cup sweet butter, softened
2 cups sugar
¼ cup unsweetened dark cocoa powder
4 large eggs
1 teaspoon vanilla extract
1½ cups plain flour
½ teaspoon baking powder
7 ounces marshmallow cream, or
   2 cups miniature marshmallows
1 cup shredded fresh coconut
1 cup chopped pecans

1. Preheat the oven to 350°.

2. In a large mixer bowl, cream together the butter, sugar, and cocoa. Add the eggs and vanilla and mix well. Add the flour and baking powder and beat for 2 minutes.

3. Spread the batter in a greased and floured 9 x 13-inch baking pan. Bake for 30 minutes.

4. While the cake is still warm, spread it with marshmallow cream, then sprinkle with the coconut and pecans.

5. Cool and frost with this modestly fattening frosting:

3 cups powdered sugar

½ cup sweet butter, softened

⅓ cup unsweetened dark cocoa powder

½ cup evaporated milk

1. Combine all the ingredients in a mixer bowl and beat till creamy.
2. Spread the frosting on top of the marshmallow cream mixture.
3. Chill for at least 1 hour before serving.

Serves 12

III. THANKSGIVING

MENU

Roast Turkey

Cornbread Dressing

Giblet Gravy

Crunchy Sweet Potato Casserole

Sweet Peas

Cranberry Salad

Katie B's Rolls *(page 256)*

Orange Slice Cake

Iced Tea *(page 252)*

•

Thanksgiving is an exalted and considerably less superstitious holiday on the Cracker calendar than New Year's Day. It is hard to get too weirdly mystical on a day given over to gluttony, football, and plotting a strategy for your Christmas shopping.

There are so many variations on the traditional fare that I'm reducing the meal to the essentials: roast turkey, cornbread dressing, and giblet gravy; sweet peas, sweet potato casserole, salad, rolls, and dessert. They're all simple, just time-consuming when prepared all at once. My personal rule of thumb is that when a visitor or mother-in-law offers to bring something, say yes and tell them what to bring. Doing the entire meal alone, unaided, will make you grouchy and resentful, and if Thanksgiving falls on the day before your period, nearly homicidal. While your nearest and dearest laugh and merrily feast, you will glower at them from behind your grease-spotted apron and wish them all dead, which pretty much undercuts the point of the day. Do yourself a favor and resign your role as chief cook and martyr and assign someone to bring dessert, and someone bread, and someone else drink, and after that, a cleanup crew so you can take an aspirin and eat your own dessert in peace.

Roast Turkey

Here is simplicity in a bird: easy to cook, easy to eat, and even mildly healthy if you don't cover it in giblet gravy once it's on your plate (I do). I usually roast a bigger bird—closer to twenty pounds than fifteen—and the recipe here is easily adjusted: just 20 percent more of everything and your bird is covered. For a few years we smoked our turkey outside in a smoker, but our daughters missed the holiday smell of roasting turkey, so I returned to roasting it inside, filling the house with the sweet smell of sage and roasting turkey, which no Yankee Candle can duplicate.

>   **One 15-pound turkey, give or take**
>   **a couple pounds**
>   **1 gallon or so salt water (½ cup salt**
>   **to 1 gallon water) for soaking**
>   **½ cup salted butter, melted**
>   **1 teaspoon ground sea salt**
>   **1 teaspoon ground black pepper**
>   **1 tablespoon poultry seasoning**
>   **1 yellow onion, peeled and**
>   **quartered**
>   **1 rib celery, with leaves**

1. The day before Thanksgiving, fill a cooler with a gallon or so of salt water and soak the turkey. (If you've procrastinated with thawing your bird and it's still frozen, then make that warm salt water.)

2. The next morning, preheat the oven to 400°.

3. Rinse the turkey and pat dry. Put it in a big roasting pan, brush with the melted butter, and sprinkle with the seasonings. Stick the onion and whole celery in the cavity. If you're into a perfectly shaped bird, truss up the legs.

4. Roast for 1 hour. Reduce the oven temperature to 250° and roast for 1½ hours. If you want a really tender breast, then cook the turkey breast down. If you want a crunchy brown breast, cook it breast up, and cook another hour. If the breast gets too brown in the last 30 minutes, put a tent of aluminum foil over it or a lid on the roaster. To tell if it's done, stick a knife in the breast. If the juices run clear (not pink), it should be done.

5. When the turkey is done, take it out of the roasting pan and put it on a serving platter. Save the pan drippings for gravy.

Serves 8

Cornbread Dressing

My aunt Doris was famous for two culinary masterpieces: her fruitcake and her corn-bread dressing, the latter being little short of legendary. I tried to duplicate it for many years but couldn't quite hit the spot. I finally went to my cousin Nelson to go over the steps and make sure I hadn't forgotten anything. As it turned out, the secret of her savory dressing is the sacrifice of an entire stewed hen in the dressing and gravy. Yes, a whole hen, so your meal will require two birds: a big one and a little one. Trust me when I say the result is worth it.

This is the basic recipe and can be made into pecan dressing, or sausage, or even oyster, if you like. Just make the basic recipe as written, but instead of giblets, toss in a cup of either chopped pecans, browned bulk sausage, or oysters. Cook just the same.

1 whole hen
1 large iron pan of cornbread, crumbled, or
    1 bag prepared cornbread crumbles,
    about 5 cups
3 slices white or wheat bread, crumbled
2 cups chopped celery
2 cups chopped yellow onion
1 tablespoon fresh sage
1 tablespoon poultry seasoning
1 teaspoon ground sea salt
1 teaspoon ground black pepper
½ cup salted butter, melted
3 large eggs, beaten
1 cup finely chopped cooked giblets

1. First off, cook down a hen. In layman's terms this means just put a hen in a large pot of water—at least 3 quarts—and cook over low heat for a few hours, till it is cooked to pieces.

2. Set it aside to cool, then pick out the bones and some of the skin. Save the leftover meat and fat and broth to make the dressing and gravy. (Nelson does his the day before or sometime earlier in the week, and refrigerates the broth so the fat will congeal on top. I don't know why he goes to the trouble, as he never actually skims the fat and throws it away, but there it is. Chilling the hen does make the boning process a little easier.)

3. Preheat the oven to 400°.

4. To make the dressing, combine the breads, vegetables, and seasonings along with the butter, eggs, and giblets in a large bowl and mix till well combined. Add 2 quarts of the hen stock and mix well for a wet, almost soupy mixture. Stir in 2 cups of the hen meat.

5. Pour the dressing into a large baking dish. Bake for 30 to 40 minutes, till brown on top. Serve with giblet gravy.

Serves 8

Giblet Gravy

This is the gravy that undercuts the nutritional lightness of the turkey, and believe me, it's worth the extra sit-ups it'll take for you to fit back into your jeans. Eat with dressing, mashed potatoes, and sliced turkey—and save the leftovers, as it is about the best gravy around. Mama claims that one year at some sort of church supper or homecoming, two brethren almost came to blows when one of them took the very last of Aunt Doris's dressing as he went down the food line, leaving an empty pan for the man behind him, who was not amused at his lack of Christian charity.

"Like to have got in a fistfight," is the way Mama explains it, with pride; glad to be affiliated with a cook of such repute.

Neck and giblets from 1 turkey
4 cups hen broth (see preceding recipe)
Fat and drippings from the bottom of
    the turkey roasting pan
¼ cup plain flour
1 cup hen meat
2 hard-boiled eggs, chopped
Salt and ground black pepper to taste

1. Cook the giblets and neck in the broth over medium heat till well done; the neck meat should be falling off the bone. Strain the stock and reserve. Chop up the giblets and cut away any loose neck meat.

2. When the turkey is finished cooking, remove it to a platter and scrape all the fat and drippings off the bottom of the roasting pan into a medium saucepan. Heat over medium-high heat. Sprinkle with the flour and cook, stirring, until the roux is light brown.

3. Stir in the reserved stock, the hen meat, chopped giblets, and hard-boiled eggs. If the gravy is too thick, add a little more broth. If it is too thin, just keep simmering on low till thickened.

4. Season with salt and a lot of black pepper to taste.

Crunchy Sweet Potato Casserole

My traditional sweet potato Thanksgiving dish is as rich as dessert and a perfect side for turkey or ham or both. The amount of butter isn't a typo. Unless your doctor has given you the lose-weight-or-die speech, I'd advise you to buy a girdle or marry one of my cousins. Our family has a great traditional acceptance of the big-boned, the hefty, and the well fed, as seen in this eighty-year-old photograph of my great-great-grandmother Candacy and my great-great-granddaddy Ben, with their daughter, son-in-law, and passel of barefoot grandchildren.

Ben and Candacy married in 1864, when he was a CSA Corporal and Candacy was somewhere in the neighborhood of thirteen (or maybe fifteen; the records vary). After the war, they returned to Alabama in a wagon and enjoyed a devoted marriage, according to the reports of my uncle Elbert, who shared a pallet with Ben when he was a little boy. As you can see, Candacy wasn't a woman who shied away from the dining table. When she died, she was so "big-boned" they had to break her legs to fit her in her coffin.

When Wendel first heard this story, he was frankly appalled and hastened to assure me (without a shred of irony) that he'd never let them break *my* legs post-mortem to fit me into *anything*. He swore he'd have my coffin custom-built if need be.

This casserole is really as rich as dessert and is especially good with something relatively bland, like turkey. Actually it's good with just about anything.

3 cups mashed cooked sweet potatoes
1 cup packed brown sugar
1 large egg, beaten
½ cup sweet butter, melted
1 tablespoon vanilla extract

TOPPING
1 cup chopped pecans
1 cup flaked coconut
1 cup packed brown sugar
¼ cup sweet butter, melted

1. Preheat the oven to 350°.
2. Mix the sweet potatoes, brown sugar, egg, butter, and vanilla in a medium bowl. Spoon the mixture into a 9 x 13-inch nonstick baking dish.
3. To make the topping, mix the pecans, coconut, brown sugar, and butter together till crumbly. Pile it on top of the potato mixture.
4. Bake 40 minutes, till the butter is sizzling around the edges.

Serves 8

Sweet Peas

If there is a prize for Easiest Dish on Earth, it is this recipe, a matter of opening a can. I retain the right to use canned goods in any Cracker recipe since a good part of our history was played out in the subtropics, without benefit of electricity. Canned goods and salted meats were our best friends.

Two 15-ounce cans young sweet peas
2 tablespoons sweet butter
Salt and ground black pepper to taste

1. Drain the liquid from the canned peas and pour the peas into a medium saucepan.
2. Add the butter and cook over medium heat till the butter is melted. Season with salt and pepper.

Serves 4 (can be doubled, or tripled, or
quadrupled, for that matter)

Cranberry Salad

I really have no idea how this most Yankee of all fruit (or is it is a vegetable?) made its way down the eastern seaboard and took precedence on the traditional Cracker Thanksgiving table. Maybe it was an article of Surrender at Appomattox that Southerners support New England by eating their produce, I don't know. I do know that I've never sat down at a Thanksgiving table that didn't have a strange little plate of congealed cranberry sauce, still shaped like the can it came out of. I never found it to be the most appetizing little dish on earth, and fortunately for all of us, a new version has taken hold in recent years. It is a little less simple to serve but worth the trouble.

Two 12-ounce packages fresh cranberries
1 cup sugar
1 pint heavy cream
One 20-ounce can crushed pineapple, drained
1 cup chopped pecans
7 ounces miniature marshmallows

1. Chop the cranberries either by hand (with a sharp knife) or in a food processor. Mix with the sugar in a large bowl and chill overnight.

2. The next morning, whip the cream and fold it into the chopped cranberries along with the pineapple, pecans, and marshmallows. Refrigerate until ready to serve.

Serves 8 and, honey, it is good

Orange Slice Cake

In the heart of Cracker Florida, oranges come to harvest around the holidays. In their honor, instead of the usual pies, I am offering the always delicious Orange Slice Cake. It's definitely a modern Cracker invention, dating back to the 1940s, when every orange grove on Highway 441, from the Georgia state line to Miami (or *My-amma*, as Crackers call it) had its own little store and book of recipes. It is a strange little cake and strangely delicious if you like little orange-slice candies (and I do).

> 1 cup sweet butter, softened
> 2 cups granulated sugar
> 4 large eggs
> 1 teaspoon baking soda
> ½ cup buttermilk
> 3½ cups all-purpose flour
> 1 pound chopped dates
> 1 pound orange-slice candies (found in
>   the candy aisle at your grocery store),
>   chopped
> 2 cups chopped pecans
> 1¼ cups grated fresh coconut

GLAZE
> 1 cup fresh orange juice
> 2 cups powdered sugar

1. Preheat the oven to 250°.

2. In a mixer bowl, cream the butter and sugar until light. Add the eggs, one at a time, and beat well after each addition.

3. Dissolve the baking soda in the buttermilk, add to the butter mixture, and blend well.

4. Place the flour in a large bowl. Add the dates, candies, and nuts and stir to coat all the pieces well.

5. Add the flour mixture and coconut to the creamed mixture and stir.

6. Press the batter into a buttered 13 x 9-inch cake pan. Bake for 2 dang hours.

7. To make the glaze, mix the orange juice and powdered sugar until smooth. Pour the glaze over the cake as soon as you pull it out of the oven. Let it stand in the pan overnight to congeal into true orange ecstasy, then cut into squares.

Serves 8 to 10

IV. CHRISTMAS COOKIE BRUNCH

If you and your friends and kin are looking for a lighthearted way to socialize in the stressful countdown till Christmas, pencil in a Christmas Cookie Brunch on a Saturday morning in early December. It is both fun and useful. Our parties generally go something like this: Everyone meets for brunch at the house of whoever has the biggest kitchen, bringing along two favorite cookie recipes, plus ingredients, with a little extra to share.

After a slice of quiche and a cup of coffee, we retire to the kitchen to bake, eat, and commiserate over fallen batter or limp divinity. Recipes are exchanged, as is pertinent holiday gossip. At the end of the brunch, all the cookies are laid out on a big table, and the participants (and even a few nonparticipants who wander in from the cold) fill their holiday Tupperware with a large and colorful assortment of cookies that can be eaten with family or given to teachers, mailmen, or neighbors as gifts.

Here's a shot of Burger (right) and our long-time partner in crime, Shari B, at our last cookie brunch, rolling out a pan of angel balls. (Incidentally, Shari is the woman I would have been sneaking off with to the funeral home to do a dye job had anything happened to Burger when we were young.) Katie B used an old-school Cracker saying to describe efficient women, "she can get the clothes on the line," meaning she didn't just begin the household washing but saw it through to the end. Well, these two can get the clothes on the line, iron those clothes and have them put away before sundown. They can also skin a buck and run a trotline—and make a heck of a quiche.

Spinach Quiche

This is the perfect brunch quiche—eggy and cheesy and with enough spinach to give it the illusion of being nutritious.

**One 10-ounce package frozen chopped spinach,
    thawed and drained**
1 bunch green onions, chopped
4 large eggs, beaten
One 16-ounce carton small curd cottage cheese
2 cups shredded sharp Cheddar cheese
One 9-inch Flaky Pie Crust (page 258)

1. Preheat the oven to 325°.

2. In a large mixing bowl, mix the spinach, onions, eggs, cottage cheese, and Cheddar cheese till well blended.

3. Pour into the unbaked pie crust and bake for 1 hour, till firm in the center.

4. Let stand for 10 minutes before cutting.

Serves 6

Hors d'oeuvre Pie

My buddy Miss Helen gave me this recipe. She isn't a Cracker by birth but Canadian (Canadian Yankees, we call them around here; a term both inaccurate and probably fighting words above the border). She has been a great audience for my stories for thirty years. When my first novel came out, another buddy of ours from church, Mr. Doug, wanted to read it, but he was blind and the book was too obscure to sell in audio. Miss Helen took the matter in hand and, over the course of many months, read it to him aloud to their equal enjoyment, as Doug was a New York Yankee who was much entertained by my Cracker *oeuvre*. I think the generosity of the gesture merits a lifetime membership to the Cracker species, something I know she has always aspired to. Her husband, Maury, is so shiftless that he is often mistaken for a Cracker anyway.

2 frozen unbaked pie crusts, thawed
One 8-ounce package cream cheese, softened
½ cup mayonnaise

TOPPING
½ cup crumbled blue cheese
3 hard-boiled eggs, chopped
1 red onion, cut into thin rings
1 cup chopped green bell pepper
1 cup broccoli florets
½ cup cherry tomatoes
½ cup sliced black olives

1. Preheat the oven to 350°.

2. Roll out the pie crusts on a large baking sheet till they are flat and bake for 7 to 10 minutes, till brown.

3. Take the pie crusts out of the oven and while they are cooling, beat the cream cheese and mayonnaise in a mixer bowl till light.

4. While the pie crusts are still warm, spread the cream cheese mixture on top as you would spread sauce on pizza dough.

5. Top with the blue cheese, chopped eggs, onion, bell pepper, broccoli, tomatoes, and black olives.

6. To serve, cut into wedges with a serrated knife.

Serves 8

Orange Chocolate Chip Muffins

Orange and chocolate are another one of those combinations that just can't go wrong. If you like your muffins less sweet, or less messy, don't dribble on the glaze.

> ¾ cup canola oil
> 1 cup granulated sugar
> 2 large eggs
> 1½ cups self-rising flour
> ½ teaspoon baking soda
> 2 tablespoons grated orange zest
> ¼ cup fresh orange juice
> 1 teaspoon vanilla extract
> 1 cup semisweet mini chocolate chips,
>   plus more for garnish

GLAZE
> ½ cup powdered sugar
> 1 tablespoon fresh orange juice
> 1 teaspoon vanilla extract

1. Preheat the oven to 350°.

2. Mix the oil, granulated sugar, and eggs in a mixer bowl until well blended. Add the flour, baking soda, orange zest, orange juice, vanilla, and chocolate chips and mix well (it should be kind of lumpy).

3. Pour the batter into a greased 12-cup muffin pan. Bake for 12 to 15 minutes.

4. To make the glaze, mix the powdered sugar, orange juice, and vanilla till smooth. Dribble it over the warm muffins and top each muffin with a few chocolate chips.

Makes 12

Angel Balls

Once your guests have stuffed themselves on brunch, they can begin the working part of the party and start rolling out those cookies. To begin, this is an odd little cookielike confection, which might even be said to be on the healthy side, comparatively speaking. The recipe doesn't double well, unless you have an army of helpers to roll them out while they're still warm. Once the mixture cools, it doesn't stick together as easily. The end result is worth the effort: chewy, crunchy, and angelically light.

1 pound chopped dates
1 cup sweet butter, softened
8 ounces shredded fresh coconut
1 cup granulated sugar
1 cup packed light brown sugar
4 cups puffed rice cereal
2 cups chopped nuts (I use pecans, but
    walnuts are good, too)
1 teaspoon vanilla extract
2 cups powdered sugar

1. Mix the dates, butter, coconut, and granulated and brown sugars in a large saucepan and cook over medium heat for 6 minutes.

2. Let cool just long enough that you can put your hands in without getting burned.

3. Stir in the cereal, nuts, and vanilla, then quickly roll into small, golf ball–sized balls.

4. Spread the powdered sugar on a countertop and roll the balls in the sugar till well coated.

5. Set on wax paper to cool.

Makes about 3 dozen

Velveeta Rocky Road Fudge

What Cracker cookbook is complete without the gothic use of Velveeta?

I think this recipe represents just the sort of collapse of rules of civilized engagement that William Faulkner feared would happen when the Snopeses moved into town. The careless mixing of cheese! Cocoa! Marshmallows! Where will it end?

But, hey, it's not only good to eat but also good as a conversation piece when people ask for the recipe. ("Yes, Velveeta, just like you put on nachos!") Don't knock it till you try it.

1 cup sweet butter, softened
8 ounces pasteurized process cheese
    product, cubed
5 cups powdered sugar
½ cup unsweetened cocoa powder
½ cup nonfat dry milk powder
2 teaspoons vanilla extract
2 cups coarsely chopped pecans
1 cup chopped miniature marshmallows

1. Heat the butter and cheese cubes together in a heavy-bottomed saucepan over medium heat, stirring to make sure it doesn't scorch, till melted.

2. Mix the powdered sugar and cocoa. Add to the cheese and mix well.

3. Stir in the milk powder, vanilla, pecans, and marshmallows. Pour the mixture into a nonstick 9-inch-square pan.

4. Chill until firm. Cut into squares with a serrated knife.

Makes 3 pounds

Orange Balls

Orange Balls are a twist on traditional rum balls, which are made the exact same way, with rum instead of orange juice. If you substitute chocolate sandwich cookies for the vanilla wafers and crème de menthe for the juice, you'll have chocolate mint balls. Feel free to tinker and adjust.

12 ounces vanilla wafer cookies, crushed
1 cup powdered sugar, plus more for coating
¼ cup sweet butter, softened
½ cup orange juice concentrate, thawed
½ teaspoon vanilla extract
1 cup chopped pecans

1. Combine the cookie crumbs and powdered sugar in a medium bowl, then stir in the butter.
2. Stir in the orange juice concentrate, then stir in the vanilla and nuts.
3. Shape the mixture into walnut-sized balls, then coat in powdered sugar.

Makes 3 dozen

Haystacks

Haystacks work well at cookie parties because they don't require baking. They are made in the microwave and are no more labor intensive than stirring and spooning.

1 cup butterscotch chips
½ cup peanut butter
½ cup Spanish peanuts
2 cups dry chow mein noodles

1. Put the chips and peanut butter in a microwavable bowl and microwave for 3 minutes at medium power, then stir.
2. Add the peanuts and noodles and toss so that the noodles are evenly coated.
3. Drop by the teaspoon onto wax paper and let harden.

Makes 3 dozen

Crazy Good Chocolate Candy Cookies

I've been making these cookies since I was in college, when I made the recipe in front of my speech class as a project and made a rare A-plus. After thirty years, it's still a praiseworthy little mixture. When my daughter Emily was a child, she would say of particularly wonderful recipes that they weren't just good, they were *crazy* good. This recipe applies.

1 cup packed brown sugar
½ cup granulated sugar
2 large eggs
1 cup sweet butter
1½ teaspoons vanilla extract
2½ cups plain flour
1 teaspoon baking soda
1 teaspoon salt
1½ cups candy-covered chocolate pieces,
      half whole, half slightly crushed
1 cup chopped pecans

1. Preheat the oven to 350°.
2. Put both sugars, the eggs, butter, and vanilla in a large mixer bowl and mix thoroughly.
3. Add the flour, baking soda, and salt and blend well. Stir in the crushed candy and pecans.
4. Drop the dough by the teaspoon onto cookie sheets and top each cookie with three or so intact candy pieces.
5. Bake for 10 minutes, till the tops are just brown.

Makes 5 dozen

Surprise Brownies

I went to Jefferson, Texas's Pulpwood Queens Girlfriend Weekend this year and came back with more than big hair—namely, this simple recipe for Surprise Brownies, which are the specialty of the house at the Delta Street Inn. I think I might have eaten one hundred of them in the course of my three-day stay. They are like all things Texan: secretive and sweet and a little addictive. The secret is in the middle layer— a bite of real chocolate that makes this ordinary little brownie divine.

One 17-ounce package commercial brownie mix
5 milk chocolate bars, plain, almond, or toffee

1. Mix the brownie mix according to the directions on the bag or box.

2. Pour half the batter into a greased and floured 9-inch-square pan.

3. Break up the chocolate bars and put the pieces on top of the batter in the pan. Pour the remaining batter on top.

4. Bake as directed. Let cool to room temperature, then cut into squares with a serrated knife.

Makes 12

Pecan Shortbread

These shortbread cookies are disarmingly simple and as easy to make as they are to eat, I'm afraid. Once I get started, I can't stop. But other than being addictive, they're a great holiday cookie and a good traveler. If you're sending a cookie box to a soldier in the desert, this one works well as long as it is packed tight. Since the cookies can be merrily decorated, they will give any gift box a festive air.

½ **cup sweet butter, softened**
⅓ **cup packed light brown sugar**
1 teaspoon real vanilla extract
⅛ **teaspoon salt**
1¼ **cups plain flour**
¾ **cup finely chopped pecans**
Flour for rolling
Holiday colored sprinkles

1. Preheat the oven to 325°.

2. Beat the butter, sugar, and vanilla together in a mixer bowl.

3. Stir in the salt and flour and then the pecans. Knead with your hands till smooth.

4. Roll the dough out on a lightly floured surface to about ¼ inch thick. Cut into shapes with a biscuit cutter or holiday cookie cutters.

5. Bake on an ungreased cookie sheet for about 20 minutes, till slightly brown on the edges.

6. Decorate with holiday sprinkles while still warm.

Makes about 1½ dozen

Divinity

Finally, in the candy department, we have that old Cracker Classic, divinity, that has caused many a devout old Grannie to cuss aloud, even in the presence of her grandchildren, and to burn up the motor on many a hand mixer. The cussing comes about because divinity is a dicey little delicacy. If you don't get your temperatures right, you end up with meringue frosting and then you have to make a whole dang cake to use it. Read carefully and go slowly. If your divinity goes flat, no worries. It's just one of those little tragedies of life that binds us together in our common humanity. If your fellow partygoers are any kind of friends at all, they'll hasten to commiserate and tell a few stories of flat divinity of their own.

4 cups sugar
1 cup white corn syrup
1 cup water
¼ teaspoon salt
3 large egg whites, at room
    temperature
1 teaspoon vanilla extract
1 cup chopped pecans

1. Stir the sugar, corn syrup, water, and salt together in a heavy saucepan and heat over medium heat till the mixture starts to boil.

2. Continue boiling until the mixture forms a soft ball when dropped in a glass of cool water (see Note on page 169).

3. In the meantime, beat the egg whites in a mixer bowl until stiff.

4. When the syrup comes to the soft-ball stage, pour ½ cup into the egg whites in a thin stream, while beating fast all the time.

5. Continue to boil the remaining syrup while beating the egg whites, until the syrup reaches the light-crack stage when dropped in cold water (that is, the soft ball becomes a hard ball).

6. Pour the remaining syrup into the egg white mixture, beating all the while. Continue beating until the candy begins to hold its shape.

7. Working quickly, stir in the vanilla and nuts. Drop by the teaspoon onto wax paper and let dry completely.

Makes 3 to 4 dozen

Note: Sugar syrup reaches the soft ball stage between 235° and 240°. Using a candy thermometer, check the temperature. When the syrup reaches 235°, use a spoon to drop a little into a glass of cold water. If the syrup forms a soft, pliable ball, it has reached the soft ball stage.

One word of caution: Be sure to use a spoon to drop the sugar syrup into the water, as the syrup is extremely hot and can burn you.

V. CHRISTMAS

●

Children, go where I send thee.
How shall I send thee? Oh!
I'm gonna send thee one by one,
One for the little bitty baby, born in Bethlehem
—TRADITIONAL CHRISTMAS SPIRITUAL

●

All things considered, Christmas is still the supreme holiday in Crackerdom, even more beloved than the first day of hunting season, or NASCAR, or even Thanksgiving. My mother tells many a warm story of how Grannie used to jump on the Marianna bus the moment her brothers gave her their annual monetary gift (and well earned; Grannie did their laundry year-round) to go downtown on Christmas Eve to buy everyone presents. She wouldn't buy just for her own children, but for all the children in the neighborhood, if they weren't getting anything else: cheap dolls, tea sets, oranges, and whatever else she came upon before the shops closed.

I think it's about time every adult in America follows her lead and does likewise to make sure our American children are getting their share before we start buying for ourselves. You might say Thanksgiving is for hunters; Fourth of July, for patriots. Christmas is for children, in honor of the little bitty baby, born in Bethlehem.

Here is a family Christmas shot taken two years before I was born (which may account for my brothers' carefree smiles).

Jay is left, Jeff a baby on my cousin Linda Ann's lap, and the unquenchable Nelson (who donated his mother's dressing recipe) on the right, smiling with cowboy pride into the camera. The cowboy outfits were courtesy of my uncle Kelly—he of the tall tales—who didn't have any children of his own and was always good for a really primo present.

My Christmas menu might seem familiar, and so it is, as the traditional Cracker Christmas dinner is actually a rerun of our Thanksgiving dinner—so jump back a chapter for how to make turkey and giblet gravy. The exception comes in the traditional side dishes—the soup to begin the meal, the Ambrosia, and to finish, a homemade Lane Cake.

Cheesy Broccoli Soup

Since Christmas Dinner often includes guests, feel free to start them out with this warm and cozy little soup, which is a nice complement to the turkey.

2 bunches fresh broccoli
1 head fresh cauliflower
4 cups chicken broth
¼ cup sweet butter
1 medium yellow onion, chopped
2 cloves garlic, minced
½ cup plain flour
4 cups whole milk
½ teaspoon dried thyme
Salt and ground black pepper to taste
12 ounces pasteurized process cheese
    product, cubed

1. Trim the broccoli and cauliflower and cut into bite-sized pieces. Combine the broccoli, cauliflower, and broth in a large pot and cook covered over medium heat until tender.

2. Heat the butter in a heavy-bottomed pot over medium heat. Add the onion and garlic and sauté until onion is transparent. Add to the broccoli mixture.

3. Mix the flour and ¼ cup of the milk in a small bowl. Add to the broccoli mixture along with the remaining 3¾ cups milk and the thyme. Season with salt and pepper.

4. Simmer uncovered over medium heat till the vegetables are tender, about 20 minutes.

5. Add the cheese and stir until it all melts in, being careful not to let it scorch.

Serves 8

Ambrosia

Ambrosia, basically just a fresh citrus salad, is beloved all over the South, and especially in orange-crazy Florida. Like most old-school dishes, it has endless variations. The only time-honored, indisputable ingredients are orange and coconut. Consider this your base ambrosia, and if you take a liking to any other fruit known to man, dice it up and give it a whirl. Brace yourself beforehand, because ambrosia is a little bit of a pain in the butt to make. The secret is to get off all that bitter white membrane, which takes a good bit of work with a sharp knife.

In the grand scheme of holiday fare, this is a rare and naturally healthy dish. It will make you healthy, high energy, and (according to Burger, who supplies me with my holiday ambrosia) regular.

Oh, and this is the recipe for a whole bag of oranges, two pounds. You can halve it for smaller portions, or make this large one, refrigerate, and eat till New Year's.

One 2-pound bag oranges
One 20-ounce can crushed pineapple,
   undrained
1 cup shredded fresh coconut
Up to ½ cup sugar or Splenda, to taste
½ cup chopped pecans
½ cup halved maraschino cherries

1. Get yourself a big bowl and peel your oranges, then section and use a sharp knife to trim off the white membrane, till they are reduced to orange pulp bliss.

2. Add the pineapple and coconut and stir to combine. Taste and add a little sugar if it's not sweet enough. Stir in the pecans and cherries, and chill.

3. Variations include adding grapes, sliced bananas, and even whipped topping, to give it a creamier texture. Some people throw in a dash of Grand Marnier or vanilla, but if your oranges are sweet and fresh (as they are in Florida during the winter), you won't need to cheat.

Serves 8

Lane Cake

Lane Cake is traditionally an Alabama cake, or so I gather (from the fact that Alabamans are the only people I know who have ever heard of it). It is Katie B's favorite, and I used to make it for her birthday in August, though it is traditionally made at Christmas. Variations abound. I ice this one with meringue frosting, though cream cheese frosting is also good. Mama doesn't frost her Lane Cake at all and looks down her nose at mine because I do.

Naked or clothed, it is a heck of a cake. For you lazy Crackers, skip the cake part and substitute a packaged white cake mix. Just between you and me, Mama cheats this way but, hey, she's eighty-two. Back in the day, she made hers from scratch.

1 cup sweet butter, softened
2 cups sugar
3 cups sifted cake flour
1 tablespoon baking powder
Pinch of baking soda
¾ cup buttermilk
2 teaspoons vanilla extract
8 large egg whites, at room temperature

1. Preheat the oven to 325°.

2. Cream the butter in a mixer bowl. Gradually beat in the sugar and continue to beat until light and fluffy.

3. Mix the flour, baking powder, and baking soda in a separate bowl. Add the flour mixture to the creamed mixture alternately with the buttermilk, beginning and ending with the flour mixture and beating after each addition. Beat in the vanilla.

4. Beat the egg whites in a second mixer bowl till stiff, then fold into the batter.

5. Pour the batter into 5 greased and floured 9-inch round cake pans, making thin layers.

6. Bake for 15 to 20 minutes, till very lightly browned (don't overcook).

7. Let cool completely in the pans. Spread the filling between the cake layers and on the top. Frost the side of the cake with meringue.

FILLING

    8 large egg yolks

    2 cups sugar

    1 cup sweet butter

    2 cups chopped pecans

    1 cup raisins

    One 20-ounce can crushed pineapple,
        drained

    ¼ cup liquor (Katie B liked bourbon;
        Mama uses rum)

1. Combine the egg yolks, sugar, and butter in a heavy saucepan. Cook, stirring constantly, over medium heat until thickened.

2. Stir in the remaining ingredients and let cool completely before assembling the cake.

MERINGUE FROSTING

    1½ cups sugar

    ¼ cup cold water

    2 large egg whites (no yolk or you're
        out of business)

    1 tablespoon light corn syrup

    1 teaspoon vanilla extract

1. Put all the ingredients except the vanilla in a mixer bowl and beat for 30 seconds, till well blended.

2. Put in the top of a double boiler or on a very low burner and beat on high speed with a hand mixer until stiff peaks form.

3. Add the vanilla and beat for another minute, till thick enough to spread.

Serves 10

Mama's Fudge

Here's yet another fudge recipe—Mama's old recipe for cooked Christmas fudge—just in case you feel you need a little more sugar in your diet. It is fun to cook with children, but be careful with the splatter and discourage finger dipping or you'll have a howling little Cracker on your hands. If you don't cook it long enough and find out at the end that it won't harden, don't throw it away, just eat it as is with a spoon or use it for topping ice cream or pound cake—or better yet, send it to me. I have no such prejudice. Where fudge is concerned, I believe in eating my failures. It's the secret of my success.

2 cups sugar
⅓ cup white corn syrup
½ cup evaporated milk
3 tablespoons unsweetened cocoa powder
⅓ stick sweet butter, melted
1½ cups pecan halves
1 tablespoon vanilla extract

1. Mix the sugar, corn syrup, evaporated milk, and cocoa in a heavy-bottomed pot and cook, with minimal stirring, over medium-high heat until a drop of it in cold water forms a soft ball, 8 to 10 minutes (see Note on page 169).

2. Remove from the heat, add the butter, and start beating with a stout (that is, wooden) spoon. Beat until thickened, then stir in the pecans and vanilla.

3. Pour immediately into a buttered 9-inch-square pan and spread it out while it's still soft.

4. Let it sit and harden if you have will power; otherwise, eat it soft.

Makes 2 pounds

Notes on the Custom of Shouting
"Christmas Gift!"

If you're an old-school Southerner, black or white or any shade in between, you are well aware of the custom of greeting people on Christmas morning with a hale and hearty "Christmas Gift!" The practice dates back to slavery and beyond and is part demand (or promise) of a present; part jolly holiday greeting, connected to the good news spread by the shepherds in Bethlehem.

In my own hotly competitive little Cracker clan, my brothers and father work very hard to say it first, I really don't know why—maybe to get an extra present. Daddy occasionally cheats by calling on Christmas Eve and wishing you a Christmas *Eve* Gift, which does him no good, as it is an obvious technical foul, and we are quick to call him on it.

If you happen to be out and about in the dear old Southland early on a frosty Christmas morning and come across any indigenous native species over sixty at a grocery store or hotel or gas station, smile and say, "Christmas Gift."

You'll get a grin in return, and the phrase echoed back in blessing or a thank you. I guarantee it.

CHAPTER FOUR

The Clear, Cold Days of Winter

Ah, January. Is there a quieter, more peaceful month on the calendar? The holiday rush is behind you; the dead Christmas tree finally rolled outside and burned on the burn pile, the pecan trees bare and lovely against a mauve evening sky. January is a shy suitor, all quiet smile and smoldering sensual charm, an antidote for the frayed nerves of December that ushers in the crisp silence of the Southern winter. Here in North Florida, our winter isn't snow-covered and monotone, but relentlessly green, all the way till Easter. Granted, the green is gray-muted and the hickories and pecan trees bare, but a drive down Highway 19 through the flat woods of Taylor County, even two weeks into January, will show signs of a spring-like awakening: unfurling palms and blooming wild red maple, defying the winter sky with a brilliant bit of early color.

So it continues through February, when the frost can (and does) fall, and even the liveliest Cracker is occasionally stuck indoors, making for a season of introspection and personal resolution that is infused with a shy aura of hope—that you'll stick to your new diet, or give up snuff, or find a date to the Valentine's Dance. The catch is that Crackers don't really *trust* anything as comforting and benign as hope, and feel the need to increase their odds of success by kicking off their New Year with something they *do* believe in: superstition.

I. NEW YEAR'S DAY

MENU

Country Ham and Red-eye Gravy

Black-eyed Peas and Hog Jowls or Texas Caviar

Grannie's Fried Greens

Pepper Sauce *(page 239)*

Deviled Eggs

Cracklin' Cornbread *(page 12)*

Key Lime Pie

Orange Pie

Iced Tea *(page 252)* or Light Lemony Iced Tea *(page 254)*

So begins the New Year on a holiday that is, without argument, the most superstition-laden day on the Cracker calendar, and offers a menu weighted with all sorts of premonitions and dire warnings, some dating back to medieval times.

Right off the top of my head, I can think of a handful of things you never want to do on New Year's Day if you're a superstitious Cracker, foremost, to have a woman cross your threshold first thing, especially a red-headed woman. The first is bad luck, the second is deadly bad luck. Mama's neighbor lady in Marianna, Miss Bridges (beloved mother of illustrious Uncle Clyde), wouldn't open her front door to a woman on New Year's Day, not even her own daughters-in-law, two of whom were redheads. She'd run them off with a broom if she had to; to do otherwise would have been childishly naive. Blood might be thicker than water, but a jinx is a jinx.

Even more deadly is washing clothes, which is tantamount to homicide, as you might wash away a loved one. When she was old, my great-aunt Emma told me how she and her sister Mae unthinkingly washed a tub of clothes on New Year's Day, 1929, six days before my father was born. When he almost died at birth, they clung to each other and wept, as they knew they were the culprits, solely responsible for the tragedy. You also can't sweep out the front door (or you'll sweep good luck away) or take out anything at all over the threshold of the front door, even garbage (same reason: taking out means you'll be losing things all year).

On the flip side, having a black-haired man cross your threshold first is considered uncommonly good luck, and even better if he is bearing gifts. And everyone knows that kissing at midnight brings good luck and love the following year, as do two common dishes, which are sold everywhere in the rural South the week after Christmas: black-eyed peas for good fortune and greens for prosperity.

I have no idea how these two particular dishes became so powerful, but far be it from me to spit in the face of tradition. For the superstitious and the hungry, here is a never-fail menu for New Year's dinner, including two sure-fire recipes for black-eyed peas. The first is a more traditional recipe; the second one was given to me by my daughter's Texas in-laws, who call it Texas Caviar. It's not really caviar at all, but a cold bean salad that offers a nice contrast to ham; so cold and delicious that it is the single item I ask them to bring to every holiday meal they attend.

Grannie's version of greens is a little less time consuming than the usual stewing method but still holds as much promise of prosperity as any other collard, mustard, or turnip green recipe. As the tradition goes, greens on the table will bring greenbacks to your wallet. Even if you don't believe in the red-haired woman or the laundry ban, you will find yourself uncommonly optimistic and full of luck after you eat this meal.

Country Ham and Red-eye Gravy

I know we've already gone through a big country ham on Easter, but the fact is that pork in any form generates many frequent-flyer miles on the Cracker calendar. This version is smaller in scope and has a slightly different gravy—old-school red-eye gravy, which is about the easiest gravy on earth to make.

Four ½-inch-thick slices country ham
1 cup cola
¼ cup brewed coffee
Freshly ground black pepper to taste

1. Heat the ham slices in a large heavy skillet over low heat until they're tender and lightly browned.

2. Add the cola to the skillet and stir to loosen all the browned bits of fat. Cook over medium heat for 5 minutes, till the ham is well heated. Stir in the coffee. The gravy won't be thick but reddish in color and grease streaked; the more grease, the better.

3. Grind a little pepper on the coated ham slices before serving but don't add salt as the ham is salty enough.

Serves 4

Black-eyed Peas and Hog Jowls

I'm starting with the traditional recipe for black-eyed peas, cooked with hog jowls or fatback. The secret is cooking them long enough that they lose their former identity as single hard peas and nearly become a soup.

2 pounds dried black-eyed peas
4 cups water
2 hog jowls
1 yellow onion, chopped
Pinch of red pepper flakes
Salt and ground black pepper to taste

1. Rinse the dried peas and soak in the water overnight.
2. When ready to cook, drain the peas and put them in a heavy-bottomed pot. Add enough water to cover and then the hog jowls.
3. Add the onion, pepper flakes, salt, and pepper. Bring to boil and boil for a few minutes. Lower the heat to medium and simmer covered for 2 hours, till the peas are tender, adding more water if necessary.
4. For a thicker consistency, mash a few peas against the side of the pot and stir in.

Serves 8

Texas Caviar

Texas Caviar has nothing to do with fish eggs but is basically a cold marinated black-eyed pea salad, and a scrumptious one at that. It is supreme-o with ham and corn-bread. If you're into multitasking, look at it this way: You have your appetite and your good luck taken care of, all in one dish.

½ **Vidalia onion, finely chopped**
½ **green bell pepper, finely chopped**
1 bunch green onions, chopped
2 cloves garlic, minced
One 8-ounce bottle Italian salad dressing
Two 15-ounce cans black-eyed peas, drained

1. Put all the ingredients in a large bowl and stir gently to combine.
2. Refrigerate for at least 2 hours but preferably overnight. This can also be served as an appetizer with tortilla chips.

Serves 5

Grannie's Fried Greens

In mainstream Southern cooking, you'll find greens stewed in fatback and water, but this is the Cracker version, called "fried greens." The end result is about the same, though fried greens were thought to be "stronger." I'm not really sure what they mean exactly by "stronger"—whether it means it has more iron and will help you plow a few extra rows, or whether frying them gives them a stronger taste.

Before you begin, you must go about the task of cleaning your greens. If they're fresh out of the ground, this will take a little effort, as little bits of grit and sand cling tenaciously to those wide green leaves and there is nothing I hate more than finding grit in my collards when I'm eating them. I feel like I'm chewing dirt (which, now that I think of it, I am). Daddy makes a whole little ceremony over going out and handpicking his greens, one leaf at a time—not too big (or they'll be tough) and not too little. Then he comes in and fills the sink with cold water and carefully peels the stems off. He dips the leaves in the cold water. When he's done baptizing the greens, he rewashes, then washes again. If you're cooking a true mess of greens, you'll have to clean a mountain of leaves, and will wonder how they'll ever fit in the pot, but no worries. They cook down quickly, and the secret of the process is patiently putting in a handful at a time. Believe me, that mountain will soon be a molehill.

Once you get them properly cleaned, greens are about the easiest vegetable on earth to cook. As far as nutrition is concerned, they're actually fairly healthy in the big picture (depending on how much bacon you fry them in). The catch is the degritting, which can be time-consuming. If you're crunched for time, Glory Mixed Greens (sold in a can) are about as close to homemade as you can get. You don't have to mess with picking and sorting and degritting, just heat and add a little crushed red pepper and you're done. Now that my children have flown the coop, on the odd night I don't feel like cooking, I send Mr. Wendel to the store for fried wings from one of the hundred-thousand local fried-chicken joints. While he's gone, I heat up a can of Glory Greens and toss in extra pepper flakes. If I'm feeling industrious, I make a pan of cornbread for the old boy (who never compliments mine as lavishly as he does my mother's).

The entire meal takes about five minutes to process and is good eating by anyone's account. I like to think the iron and fiber and good stuff from the greens balances the bad caloric karma from the chicken wings.

Then again, I like to think of myself as looking like I did when I was sixteen; so don't go by me.

2 pounds collards or mustard greens,
    thoroughly washed, drained, and
    stems and center ribs removed
8 ounces bacon
½ teaspoon red pepper flakes
1 cup water
Salt and ground black pepper to taste

1. Once your greens are duly washed, fry the bacon in a cast-iron Dutch oven till crisp, then crumble it in the pan.

2. Turn the heat under the pan to medium-high. Start tossing in the greens, a few handfuls at a time, stirring to make sure they don't burn. Sauté till they cook down, then add another handful of greens till you're out of greens.

3. Add the red pepper flakes and a little water if you want pot likker for your cornbread, which is the happy by-product of a mess of greens.

4. Simmer covered for about 15 minutes. Season with salt and pepper.

Serves 5

Deviled Eggs

Deviled eggs are the classic accompaniment to fried chicken or baked ham, though Mama makes them for any sit-down meal, or at least any meal that my youngest daughter, Isabel, attends (Mama's deviled eggs are her favorite food on earth). The eggs are so celebrated in Southern cooking that specially made little crystal egg dishes are frequent wedding gifts for young Cracker brides, all built for the enjoyment and presentation of the simple deviled egg.

6 hard-boiled eggs, peeled and cut
    lengthwise in half
¼ cup mayonnaise
2 tablespoons minced onion
2 tablespoons minced dill pickle
¼ teaspoon pickle juice
⅛ teaspoon salt
¼ teaspoon ground black pepper
½ teaspoon dried dill

1. Remove the egg yolks from the whites and put the yolks in a medium bowl. Mash with a fork till smooth.

2. Add everything but the dried dill and stir well. Fill the empty egg whites with the mixture. If you're taking them to a public function, sprinkle them lightly with dried dill, which will lend a slightly dill taste and pleasing color variation. It will send a message to friend and foe alike that you're a Cracker who knows your way around a spice cabinet.

Makes 12

Key Lime Pie

Key Lime Pie is in reality a very close cousin of what inland Crackers call Icebox Lemon Pie. It hit a wave of popularity in the sixties and today there are as many versions are there are lime seeds, with all sorts of weird variations (cream cheese, meringue, and so on). The original recipe was 100 percent pure Conch (that is, Key West Cracker) and prized because it could be made with stored ingredients on hand, including canned milk, that didn't have to be shipped in from the coast.

Key limes are easy to grow, and when they come in bloom, they will keep you in enough limes to feed North America. They're slightly smaller than Persian limes and rounder and maybe a little tangier. You can buy Key lime juice commercially, but who knows if it's the real item, and usually it's a little on the expensive side. If you're in a hurry or pinched for a dollar, I'd just use regular lime juice and let everyone assume what they will. Old-school Crackers (and Conchs) eat it naked, with no topping at all. Don't worry if the custard isn't lime green but pale yellow. That's the way God and the Conchs intended.

½ cup fresh Key lime juice
4 teaspoons grated lime zest
2 large egg yolks
One 14-ounce can sweetened condensed milk
Graham Cracker Crust (page 259)
Whipped topping (optional)

1. Preheat the oven to 350°.

2. In a mixer bowl, beat the lime juice, lime zest, and egg yolks until smooth. Add the condensed milk and beat until thickened.

3. Fill the crust with the lime mixture. Bake for 15 minutes, till the center is set.

4. Let cool, then refrigerate till cold. If you're a fan of whipped cream in any form (as I am), top with whipped cream or whipped topping to cut some of the sweetness.

Serves 6

Orange Pie

I actually think this Orange Pie is as good as Key Lime Pie, though it's never had as good PR. It is a sweet, unassuming little pie. Just because it's never made the best-seller list, don't sell it short. Many fine works of art never become bestsellers. Reject the cattle call of corporate America celebrity worship. Make this pie, and while you're eating it, read one of my novels.

Celebrate obscurity. It's the Cracker Way.

3 large egg yolks
½ cup sugar
2 tablespoons plain flour
1 tablespoon sweet butter, melted
1 tablespoon grated orange zest
1 cup fresh orange juice
One 9-inch Flaky Pie Crust (page 258)

MERINGUE
    3 large egg whites
    6 tablespoons sugar

1. Preheat the oven to 350°.
2. Put the egg yolks in a mixer bowl and beat until smooth. Beat in the sugar, flour, butter, orange zest, and orange juice, one ingredient at a time.
3. Pour the orange mixture into the pie shell. Bake for 30 minutes, till set.
4. Let cool completely. You can top the pie with sweetened whipped cream or meringue.
5. To make the meringue, beat the egg whites until foamy. Gradually beat in the sugar, and continue to beat on high speed till stiff peaks form. Spread the meringue over the pie, covering it completely. Bake for 10 minutes, until the meringue is golden brown. (And again, keep an eye on that baby or it'll burn.)
6. Chill before serving.

Serves 6

II. IN CELEBRATION OF SOUL

MENU

Yer Basic Smothered Pork Chop

Basic Baked Sweet Potatoes

Katie B's Corn Casserole

Hoecake

Buttermilk Pie

Iced Tea *(page 252)*

Given our track record with race, I think it's high time Crackers give honor to whom honor is due and admit that African Americans cook at least as good as we do—something my mother has always believed to be true. Thursday was our grocery day when I was growing up, and possibly the biggest day of the week. Mama would wear the same dress every week—a pale blue shepherd's print shift (her "grocery store dress," we called it). I remember standing at the meat case in the Winn-Dixie when I was ten or eleven, and Mama checking out the passing cart of a black lady en route to the cashier, which was full of ham and beans and collards, and commenting dryly, "I wish I was eating supper with *her.*"

The truth is, despite our very spotty history—loving and vicious—African Americans are our kinsmen, both culturally and religiously. They are the only people on earth who share our passion for church and barbecue and family, whose grandmothers also wallpaper their bedrooms with portraits of Jesus.

So closely tied are our roots and heritage that black people who glance at my index might be a little provoked at seeing a white woman claim such soul staples as fried greens and cornbread and sweet potatoes. (What's next? We also invented hip-hop and jazz?) I understand their concern, but the fact is that Soul Food and Cracker

Cooking are very closely related, like first cousins whose children marry each other. The same forces that shaped Cracker cooking—poverty and ingenuity not least—shaped soul food. Since we all started out in the South, we stewed, fried, and roasted the same little animals in the same little herbs.

The only major difference I can think of between Soul Food and Cracker Cooking is the sugar-in-cornbread debate, which has caused so many hard feelings over the years that I won't belabor it. Crackers often quote the old saw, "Cake has sugar, cornbread don't." I'm sure pro-sugar people have their own saw, and equally sure there is a no-sugar black folk contingency out there somewhere, who bristle at the idea of sweet cornbread being an African American invention. So, enough.

Martin Luther King, Jr.'s birthday falls on January 15, and I offer up this soul-inspired menu in his honor, and for all the rest of the heroes of the Movement: John Lewis and Ralph Abernathy and every single Yank, Jew, Episcopal pacifist, and student agitator among them. When they put their lives on the line and agitated Jim Crow into oblivion, they freed not only the people of color but also the children of the oppressor, who inherited the gift of diversity and eventually learned a better way (or at least some of them did; *I* did). It's a favor that can't be forgotten and won't be, not if this Cracker has anything to do with it.

Yer Basic Smothered
Pork Chop

If I had time, I would do a complete book on pork alone, call it Gone With the Oink, and make a million. But for now this simple pork chop dish will have to suffice. Eat these smothered pork chops on smashed red potatoes or rice. Or if you're alone in the house, go native and just stand at the stove and eat with your hands, the gravy running down your arms. You can take a bath when you're done.

Who'll be the wiser?

**2 tablespoons oil (olive oil is fine here, and then you
       can be proud you used the good oil for once)
4 center-cut pork chops, ½ inch thick
2 tablespoons plain flour
1 yellow onion, chopped
½ cup water
½ cup sour cream
½ cup whole milk
1 teaspoon seasoning salt
½ teaspoon ground black pepper**

1. Heat the oil in a cast-iron skillet over medium heat. Add the pork chops and cook, covered for most of the time and turning once, till they are done completely with no pink inside.

2. Remove the pork chops to a plate. Sprinkle the flour on the still-hot grease and cook, stirring, till it's a medium dark brown.

3. Toss in the onion and cook till it's a little wilted (say, a minute). Carefully stir in the water, then the sour cream, milk, salt, and pepper. Cook, stirring, for about 5 minutes. If the consistency is too thick, add a little more liquid (water or milk in this recipe).

4. When it's as thick as you like it, put your pork chops back in the pan and cook another 5 minutes or so to set the flavors.

Serves 4

Basic Baked Sweet Potatoes

Nowadays, sweet potatoes are sold fresh and washed in the produce section, or in convenient cans, ready to eat. While we're celebrating soul food, do yourself a favor and go out and get yourself a copy of Ralph Ellison's *Invisible Man*. Ellison writes a rhapsody to buying sweet potatoes on the street in the urban north, proving that he was not only a great American writer, but also a man who knew his yams.

4 fresh sweet potatoes
½ cup sweet butter, melted
4 tablespoons brown sugar
½ cup chopped pecans

1. Preheat the oven to 325°.

2. Scrub the potatoes and put them on a cookie sheet. Bake for 1 hour, just like you do baked potatoes, either wrapped in foil (for a softer jacket) or bare for a more chewy shell.

3. Poke a fork in them after an hour, and if they're hard, bake for another 30 minutes.

4. When they're tender, take them out of the oven. Split them and top with butter, brown sugar, and a few chopped pecans. Eat hot. They are especially good with pork and are the classic accompaniment for roast possum (not kidding there; ask anyone who knows possum).

Katie B's
Corn Casserole

Depression-era Crackers fell in love with a few modern conveniences: fans, Coca Cola, BC Powders, and Jiffy Corn Muffin Mix—the latter of which isn't an old-school Cracker recipe but the brainchild of an industrious Michigan Yankee. The recipe below is as close to sweet cornbread as I can get, courtesy of Katie B. It is really just a variation on spoonbread, full of old Cracker favorites like clabbered milk (sour cream), butter, corn, and more butter.

I use pure butter (never margarine and I mean never). If you're kin to someone with a cow who still presses it fresh, then ingratiate yourself to that person and make him your best friend, because fresh butter will improve the taste of any recipe in this book to the power of ten. This is a recipe of the highest caliber and is capable of sealing your reputation as a good cook, which I have found covers a multitude of sins. Eat this with sweet iced tea and greens and pork chops. It will cure what ails you.

½ cup sweet butter, melted
1 cup sour cream
One 14-ounce can cream-style corn
One 14-ounce can whole kernel corn
       (or 2 cups fresh if you can get it)
2 large eggs, beaten
One 8.5-ounce box Jiffy Corn Muffin Mix

1. Preheat the oven to 350°.
2. Put all the ingredients in a large mixing bowl and mix well.
3. Pour into a 9 x 13-inch pre-greased baking pan. Bake for 50 minutes, until golden brown.

Serves 6 to 8

Hoecake

I'm including hoecake in my Soul Food menu, as it is both delicious and historic, the invention of enterprising (and starving) field hands, who cooked it on a heated hoe in a field, hence the name. Since it's fried, you really don't have to butter it, unless you're kin to me, and have embraced our family credo, "A life without butter really isn't much of a life at all."

1½ cups plain cornmeal
½ cup self-rising flour
1 teaspoon baking powder
Pinch of salt
2 large eggs, beaten
1½ cups buttermilk
2 tablespoons canola oil

1. Stir the dry ingredients together in a mixing bowl. Add the eggs and buttermilk and whisk till smooth.

2. Heat the oil in an iron pan or griddle over medium-high heat. Pour a pancake-sized (or smaller) bit of batter in the skillet and fry like a pancake. Turn it over when it starts to bubble on the edges, then fry the other side.

3. Repeat until all the batter is used.

Serves 5

Buttermilk Pie

This modest little treasure of a pie is actually a variation of Chess Pie. I often sprinkle it with toasted coconut or pecans (or both) before serving, which makes for a crunchier pie. My husband could eat a whole one in a sitting. If you're having company over you especially like, add a dollop of whipped cream to create that trifecta of taste: creamy pie, crunchy topping, and cold, sweet cream. *Ahhh.*

Dessert doesn't get much better than this.

½ cup sweet butter, softened
1½ cups sugar
3 tablespoons plain flour
¼ teaspoon salt
3 large eggs
1 cup buttermilk
1 teaspoon grated lemon zest
One 9-inch Flaky Pie Crust (page 258)
¼ cup shredded coconut or chopped pecans,
        toasted (optional)

1. Preheat the oven to 385°.
2. Cream the butter, sugar, flour, and salt together in a mixer bowl.
3. Add the eggs, buttermilk, and lemon zest and beat till smooth.
4. Pour the egg mixture into the pie shell. Bake for 25 minutes, till the center is set.
5. Sprinkle with coconut before serving.

Serves 5

III. PIG-PICKEN TIME

MENU

One Roasted Pig

Dry Rub Ribs

Wendel's Secret Yellow Sauce

Basic Mild Red Sauce

Brunswick Stew

Brown Sugar Baked Beans

Old-school Cole Slaw

Sister Wilson's Marinated Cole Slaw

Fresh Apple Cake

Brown Sugar Cake

●

Now Crackers love pigs for both their bacon and their companionship, as is demonstrated by my brother Jay, previously shown posed with a dead deer. He is four years older than I and owns a meat market in Ocala. Old Jaybird is a Cracker of some distinction, with the usual characteristics (big truck, arsenal of guns, three hunt clubs). Though shy as a child, he has blossomed in his middle age and now has a story for every occasion. A couple of years ago, Mama had (to her complete satisfaction) a mild heart attack that put her in the hospital for a few days. Jay lives closest to her and is the family's first-response unit. As we sat in her room at Monroe Regional, waiting on the doctor, he passed the time telling me about a pig my niece Logan was raising for the FFA (Future Farmers of America) fair. She kept the old boy in a pen at the back end of their property, and for some reason (this was never properly explained), Jay got in the habit of wrestling him when he went down to feed him every afternoon.

Well, pigs are social creatures, and this one very much enjoyed the daily tussle. According to Jay (who acted the story out with great expression), when the pig would hear the hum of his diesel truck, he'd perk up his ears, run to the fence, stand on his hind hooves, and let out a mighty squeal of welcome (or challenge; don't know which). Jay would shout back and jump into the pen and the match would begin, a regular barnyard WWF. He'd throw him around and pin him and get him in full nelsons and so forth, to their mutual Cracker-pig satisfaction.

So it went for a few happy months till the little pig grew to full hog status. Logan's FFA sponsor called him at work one day and told him: "Mr. Johnson, you need to quit wrestling that pig. You're making it too aggressive. We couldn't get in the pen to weigh it."

Jay is his father's son where good manners are concerned and hastened to apologize. That was the end of the evening pig tussles.

I listened to this story, as I do most of his tales, with a face of interest (and amazement) and after a moment's consideration, asked, "What'd the pig do?"

Jay crossed his arms and with a face of mild resignation, told me, "Oh, he was disappointed at first, but then he forgot." He paused, and then added, "You know *pigs.*"

Well, I guess I do know them, as his story made perfect sense to me. I rather pitied the old porker out back, who was denied his daily pinning.

Aside from their wrestling abilities, the really valuable thing about pigs is their utter usefulness, as everything about them is usable or edible, or both. In Cracker world, they're eaten stem to stern; everything but the *oink,* as the old folk used to say. Even their hides were made into belts and their bristles into brushes. A friend of mine at UF, who was raised on a farm in LaCrosse, swore his uncles ate the fresh eyeballs during a hog killing, like popcorn at a movie, but you'll find no recipe of the sort here.

I have to draw a line somewhere.

But everything else, from the bristles, to the intestines, to the cloven feet, and comical curly tail are used, making the pig not only a dish but an all-around natural resource. You don't have to worry about disposing of industrial waste, because there isn't any. Even the head—snout, lips, and eyebrows—can be made into souse, or head cheese.

Winter was traditionally pig-killing season, from late December to mid-February. Low temperatures were needed for natural refrigeration, so pigs could be killed and preserved with salt and stored away in the smokehouse without going bad. But in these days of refrigeration, pigs are raised and killed just about round the clock. A pig-picken is no longer a prisoner of cold weather but is still generally done in the cooler months, since roasting a pig is hot work. And that's really all a pig-picken is: a barbecue where a young pig is roasted communally by a couple (or a group) of happy Cracker men, who sit on lawn chairs around the fire pit drinking iced tea or beer, and who gaily insult their sister when she comes out to check on them.

A small hog takes about eight hours to cook, first on one side, then on the other. Since we eat everything (truly), we wash the hog skin because it turns into a big solid shell of roasted cracklings and is as good as the meat inside. When the pig is duly roasted, you pick off the different parts in big chunks of meat, then chop them up and eat with whatever kind of sauce you swear by. Again, the only rule is that there are no rules. For instance, real barbecue snobs go on and on about how you should never, ever, cook sweet tomato-based sauce over a fire because the sugar will burn. Well, the truth is that Daddy always made ribs that way, charred to sweet perfection, and that's the way I like them still. When I'm presented with naked pork ribs, no matter how tender or well rubbed, I will frown and sniff at such mindless knee-bending to the snooty snobs of the world.

So don't sweat the details. Roast pork, no matter how it's prepared, is pretty ding-dang good, and rosemary with pork is an especially happy marriage. Test, tinker, and taste. If you're really new to roast pork, you might want to start out small with a couple of cheap Boston butts (which go on sale for 99 cents a pound in these parts), then work your way up to a whole pig, as a real pig-picken is fun but a commitment of time.

But, hey, if you've got a day off and a lot of hungry people, it might become a family tradition. If you live close to North Florida, call and invite me. I'll bring a cake.

One Roasted Pig

We're jumping in feet first here with a whole roasted pig, an entire day given to cooking, and at least one good pair of heatproof gloves. Look on this as an adventure in pork.

> **One 60- to 80-pound pig**
> **2 tablespoons each paprika, garlic salt,**
> **dried rosemary, ground black pepper,**
> **chili powder, and brown sugar for the rub**
> **Wendel's Secret Yellow Sauce (page 204) and/or**
> **Basic Mild Red Sauce (page 205)**

1. First off, call your local butcher or cold storage and order a trimmed pig in the 60- to 80-pound range. Unless you have a spit that revolves, get it butterflied so it can lay flat on the grill.

2. Once you get your hands on the pig, lay it out on the counter and give it a good rub with your spices. All you're doing with the rub is giving the outside skin a little flavor, so don't sweat the small print.

3. To roast a pig this size, you have to have either a very expensive smoker (we do) or a big hole in the ground and a metal grill of some sort to lay over the charcoal. If you have a professional smoker, then go by the manufacturer's instructions. If you're doing it in the ground, just keep in mind that you'll want your coals hot for 9 consecutive hours, so plan accordingly and stockpile your wood and coal.

4. At least 2 hours before you begin roasting, dig a fire pit a few feet deep, then fill with 20 pounds of coal. Light it whichever way you like (blowtorch, lighter fluid, and so on) and keep the flame going till the coals are nice and gray and hot.

5. Rake the coals around to even out the heat, then put some sort of grill over the fire pit (or the spit over it if you're a pro) and put your pig on to roast.

6. Sit around and drink iced tea or Budweiser and swap stories while you replenish the coals, keeping your heat steady, and tossing in a little oak or hickory if you prefer a woody scent.

7. Cook on the skin side for the first 4 hours, then flip the pig and cook on the other side for 3 hours. Turn it again and cook for 1 hour.

8. If you really can't tell if your pig is done, then stick a meat thermometer in a thick part of the ham. If it's over 170°, you're done. It's better to be safe than sorry because underdone pork can make you sicker than a dog and even kill you (so my mother says).

9. Once your pig is roasted, you can either leave it on the grill and let people cut (or point and you cut) what they want, or take it off the fire with a good set of thick thermal gloves, take it to a counter, let it sit a while, and pull it yourself.

10. Pulling pork is another wonderfully inexact Cracker art: Just yank off the meat in big roastlike chunks, then gently pull it apart, keeping the gloves handy, or that old pig will work out his revenge for being roasted by burning the skin off your palms.

11. When it's all pulled, put it in big disposable aluminum pans and serve with sauce, usually at least two. Save the leftovers for chopped pork sandwiches or Brunswick Stew.

Serves a whole lot of hungry Crackers;
about 2 per pound

Oh, and once your pig is off the fire, be sure and fill the fire pit with water and put it out completely, or one of the young'uns or a hungry dog might come sniffing around and step on a hot coal. They'll howl and you'll spend your evening sitting in the ER with a squalling child, or the vet's office with a squalling dog. When you get home, your wife will chew you out on top of it, and ugly references will be made to your antecedents and skill in the art of barbecue.

Dry Rub Ribs

This is basically the same recipe as the one used for the whole pig. Just reduce the spices down and don't bother digging a fire pit, but cook on your grill—propane or charcoal or wood.

> **1 teaspoon each paprika, garlic salt,**
> **dried rosemary, ground black pepper,**
> **chili powder, and brown sugar for the rub**
> **2 slabs baby back ribs**
> **Basic Mild Red Sauce (page 205; optional)**

1. Combine the dry rub ingredients and rub onto the ribs, the way you rub Ben Gay into your shoulder when it's sore.

2. Cook on the grill over low heat for the first hour, covered with either a lid or aluminum foil. Move to the hotter part of the grill and uncover. Cook, singeing the ribs, till the meat is almost falling off the bone.

3. If you like ribs sweet and crunchy, put on a coat of red sauce about 10 minutes before you take them off the grill or simply brush on a coat of honey.

Serves 4

Wendel's Secret Yellow Sauce

To make this basic mild yellow sauce hot, add cayenne pepper in small increments, till it's as hot as you want it. Wendel's secret sauce (secret no more) has about twice as much vinegar as other yellow sauces, and he has gotten a little hoity-toity in his old age and now uses red wine or balsamic vinegar. His is a little too mustardy-vinegary for my taste, but if you like the bite, then give it a whirl.

1 cup yellow mustard
¼ cup vinegar
⅓ cup packed brown sugar
2 tablespoons butter
1 tablespoon Worcestershire sauce
1 teaspoon hot sauce

1. Combine all the ingredients in a medium saucepan and simmer for 30 minutes over medium heat.

2. To make it hotter, add ½ teaspoon cayenne pepper with the hot sauce.

Makes 2 cups

Basic Mild Red Sauce

I think the whiskey in this recipe is just an excuse to bring another bottle into the house, but oh, well. The ketchup gives it a faint tomato flavor and makes for a pretty smooth little sauce. Honey can be substituted for brown sugar if you prefer the taste of honey, and it can be heated up with ½ teaspoon cayenne pepper.

2 tablespoons butter
1 cup minced yellow onion
1 clove garlic, minced
½ cup whiskey
½ cup catsup
2 teaspoons brown sugar
¼ cup white vinegar
2 teaspoons prepared mustard

Melt the butter in a deep saucepan over medium heat. Add the onion and garlic and sauté until the onion is softened. Add the remaining ingredients and simmer over medium-low heat for 30 minutes.

Makes 2 cups

Brunswick Stew

The theories of origin for this little stew are as varied as the theories about Crackers themselves. I tend to think it came from Georgia, as Georgia Crackers claim it fiercely, and since their college football teams are so inferior to Florida ones, I hate to take it away from them. (Just a little in-family teasing here, old sons. My mother is Georgian by birth and a fourth of my cousins are of the bulldawg persuasion, and despite our best efforts, remain that way till this day. We've tried the usual remedies: beatings, hypnotism, exorcism, but no dice.)

My cousin Johnny is a barbecue judge (truly, he went to school to become one), and his own signature Brunswick stew takes three days to make. He has a meat-cooking day, a stock-cooking day, then a consummation day when they're combined in a pot to simmer happily ever after. This isn't his recipe—that's locked up in a vault, I expect—but is a pretty dang good imitation. Believe me, there are as many Brunswick stew recipes as there are Crackers.

Look, consider, and toss in whatever sounds good. I like my stews to be on the tomatoey side, and if I have any ripe tomatoes around, I throw in another cup of that. Pepper flakes will make it spicier, but go easy or you'll make it too hot for the young'uns and the old folk.

1 pound chicken, cooked and diced
1 pound pork, cooked and diced
Three 14-ounce cans chicken broth
1 teaspoon ground black pepper
2 teaspoons hot sauce, or to taste
1 tablespoon Worcestershire sauce
3 to 4 tablespoons bacon drippings
½ cup barbecue sauce
1 cup catsup
1 large Vidalia onion, coarsely chopped
3 cups diced red potatoes
Three 14-ounce cans cream-style corn
1 teaspoon salt

1. Combine the chicken, pork, and chicken broth in a large pot and bring to a lively simmer. Add the remaining ingredients and simmer covered for at least 1 hour, until hot and bubbly.

2. Taste and adjust the seasonings with salt and hot sauce.

Serves 8 to 10

Brown Sugar Baked Beans

This is another recipe courtesy of my sister-in-law Jeana (wife of Jay, the Hog Wrestler), who is a cook of some repute, though she has gone distressingly skinny on us in middle age. I'm sure her cooking has suffered for it. Her baked beans were famous back in the day of the weekly Johnson barbecue, and I still cook them today.

Two 16-ounce cans pork and beans
2 tablespoons brown sugar,
    plus more for sprinkling
½ teaspoon dry mustard
½ cup catsup
1 large yellow onion, chopped
8 ounces thick-sliced bacon

1. Preheat the oven to 350°. Spray a 9 x 11-inch baking dish with nonstick spray or you'll have a devil of a time cleaning it.

2. Combine all the ingredients except the bacon in a large bowl and stir to blend.

3. Pour into the prepared pan and lay strips of bacon on top, end to end. Sprinkle with a little more brown sugar.

4. Bake for 45 minutes to 1 hour, till the bacon is nice and crisp.

Serves 5

Old-school Cole Slaw

Since the pork at pig-pickens is so hot and smoky, the usual side dishes are variations on cold salads that are light and festive and can be made in advance. Here are a few, and they can be tossed together for almost any other Cracker feast: fish fries, church suppers, you name it. To begin is the standard recipe for cole slaw, once a delicacy, but now as common in the South as gnats in August.

½ cup regular or light mayonnaise
2 tablespoons white vinegar
1 teaspoon sugar
Salt and ground black pepper to taste
Pinch of celery seeds
4 cups finely shredded cabbage
⅓ cup grated carrot
1 tablespoon finely chopped green onion
    (optional)

Put all the ingredients in a large bowl and mix. Chill for at least 1 hour. Some people like to add chopped green onion, but you have to be careful, or it'll overwhelm the cabbage and taste like onion slaw.

Serves 6

Sister Wilson's Marinated Cole Slaw

A lady at our church named Sister Wilson used to bring this version of cole slaw to church suppers. It doesn't have mayonnaise and is sweeter and slightly marinated and really good cold.

1 cup sugar
¼ cup water
¼ cup white vinegar
4 cups finely shredded cabbage
½ teaspoon celery seeds

1. In a medium saucepan, bring the sugar, water, and vinegar to a boil.
2. In a large mixing bowl, combine the shredded cabbage and celery seeds. Pour in the marinade and toss well.
3. Cover and refrigerate for at least 2 hours but preferably overnight.

Serves 6

Fresh Apple Cake

After eating all that low-fat cabbage, I know you'll be ready for dessert. Here are a couple to choose from, or make both if you're so inclined. They're masterpieces in their own way, and in Cracker idiom, will "make your tongue slap your brain."

The first is a fresh apple cake that a neighbor of mine by the name of Ruby Wells used to make. Ruby went to our church and was half Cherokee and famous for her kindly treatment of the apple. I once had a Cracker farmer friend, Danny H, come over and bulldoze a leaning laurel oak away from my house. Like most Crackers, he hates to take money from a friend and, in payment, asked for one of these cakes.

Based on the estimate I'd gotten from a tree surgeon, I'd say this cake is worth $1,200 and change.

3 cups self-rising flour
1 teaspoon baking soda
Pinch of salt
2 teaspoons ground cinnamon
3 large eggs
2 cups packed brown sugar
1½ cups vegetable oil
3 cups peeled and chopped apples,
    a firm variety, like Rome
1 cup chopped pecans, plus more
    for garnish
2 teaspoons vanilla extract

1. Preheat the oven to 325°.
2. Sift the flour, baking soda, salt, and cinnamon together into a large bowl.
3. Beat the eggs in a mixer bowl till frothy. Add the sugar and oil and beat for 3 minutes.
4. Gradually stir in the sifted dry ingredients.
5. Fold in the apples, pecans, and vanilla.

6. Pour the batter into a buttered 9 x 13-inch cake pan. Bake for 20 to 25 minutes, till firm on the top.

7. Take the cake out of the oven, poke a dozen or so holes in it with the handle of a butter knife, and pour on the glaze while the cake is still warm. Sprinkle a few more pecan pieces over the top.

GLAZE

   1 cup packed light brown sugar
   ¼ cup buttermilk
   ½ cup sweet butter
   1 teaspoon vanilla extract

1. Combine all the ingredients in a saucepan and cook over medium-high heat for 3 minutes, till bubbling around the edges.

2. Take off the heat and beat with a hand mixer till glossy. Pour over the cake while it's still warm.

Serves 9

Brown Sugar Cake

One of my beloved aunt Izzy's signature cakes, Brown Sugar Cake is bursting with pecans and character and can be used as a base for other nut and berry cakes (raisin and pecans, walnuts and pecans, candied cherries and pecans). Just substitute and play around till you create your *own* signature cake. And the amount of brown sugar isn't a typo. It really uses a whole box.

Some people frost this cake with butterscotch frosting, but I let the pecans speak for themselves. They have a lovely voice.

1 cup sweet butter, softened
½ cup vegetable shortening
1 pound light brown sugar
    (an entire pound box)
½ cup granulated sugar
3 cups self-rising flour
1 teaspoon baking powder
½ teaspoon salt
5 large egg yolks, beaten
1 cup buttermilk
2 teaspoons vanilla extract
Dash of rum or brandy
    (optional)
2 cups chopped pecans

1. Preheat the oven to 325°.
2. Cream the butter, shortening, and both sugars together in a mixer bowl.
3. Sift the flour, baking powder, and salt together in a separate bowl.
4. Add the egg yolks to the butter mixture and mix well on low speed. (Save the whites for your next meringue.)
5. Add the dry ingredients to the batter, 1 cup at a time, alternating with the but-

termilk and mixing well after each addition. Add the vanilla, rum, and pecans and stir till well blended.

6. Pour the batter into a 20-cup nonstick tube pan. Bake for 1 hour, till a toothpick inserted in the top comes out clean.

7. Remove from the pan and let cool before serving.

Serves 8

IV. HEARTY WINTER BREAKFAST

MENU

Grits and Butter

Homemade Sausage

Dirty Scrambled Eggs

Roy's Famous Biscuits

Tomato Gravy

Chocolate Gravy

Melon Slices

Perfect Coffee *(page 255)*

Crackers have always been big breakfast eaters, dating back to their days as farmers who needed a giant boost of energy to get through a long back-breaking day of labor. My father has made an art of his breakfast feasts and has gone so far as to donate to this collection detailed instructions for making his famous biscuits, typed by his own eight-fingered hands (he lost two to a wood-cutting accident when he was a child). He does not guarantee the results unless you slavishly adhere to his directions, so keep that in mind as you read along, but never fear, he is lavish in his directions.

Grits and Butter

Grits were formerly eaten round the clock in Cracker life, but now they are mostly eaten only at breakfast. There is nothing to making them—just remember to put in your salt while they're still boiling—and they are easy to customize. If you like your grits stiff, add less water. If you like them looser (so they have to be served in a bowl), then add more. Put in your pepper when they're almost done and a good portion of butter before serving, so they have a pleasing little pond of melted butter on top.

3 cups water
1 teaspoon salt
2 cups dry grits
½ teaspoon freshly ground black pepper
½ cup salted butter

1. Put the water and salt in a medium pot and heat to boiling.
2. Pour in the dry grits, then stir and turn the heat down to low.
3. Simmer covered for 15 to 20 minutes, stirring occasionally to make sure they don't stick.
4. Stir in the pepper and top with butter before serving.

Serves 6

Notes on Hominy

I think my father is the only Cracker left in creation who still eats hominy, which is dried corn soaked in (brace yourself) lye to soften it and bring out the little kernel and give it (I guess) a pleasing lye taste. I read somewhere that the Cherokee were great fans of hominy, and Daddy is part Cherokee, so maybe he got it from them. Now it's sold by the can. Since its preparation requires a long soak in lye (which can kill you), I'll take the safer road here and recommend the canned version, which can be found in the vegetable aisle of your local grocery store. It will do nicely if you really just can't live without that hominy. Just open the can, pour it into a saucepan, and heat. Hominy is not just for breakfast but is also eaten with seafood and ham.

Homemade Sausage

In Mama's youth (and even my own) people used to make their own private store of sausage, and it's really a fairly easy proposition. Jimmy Dean makes a doggone good sage sausage, but if you make it yourself, you retain bragging rights. Think how lofty and esoteric you'll sound when you tell your guests they're eating lime-sage-fusion sausage, or apple-sage-fusion, or rosemary-sage, and so on, when all you're really doing is serving them ground pork with a little bit of spice and flavor.

2 pounds lean ground pork
1 teaspoon salt
½ teaspoon dried sage
1 teaspoon freshly ground black pepper
¼ teaspoon red pepper flakes
   (or not, if you like mild)

1. Combine all the ingredients in a large bowl and mix with your hands till it is thoroughly blended.

2. Shape into 12 to 15 wide, thin patties. Brown in a cast-iron skillet for a few minutes on each side, making sure that the center is completely done.

Serves 5

Dirty Scrambled Eggs

Dirty scrambled eggs are good with grits and are sometimes served together (Grits and Eggs). To make them, cook your eggs in the same hot frying pan you just cooked your sausage. The result will be "dirty eggs"—dirty from the pork grease, and altogether wonderful. Salt and pepper, and if you like cheese and have some handy, throw on a little cheese. Then you'll have Dirty Scrambled Cheddar Eggs to serve with your fusion sausage.

6 large eggs, beaten
Sausage drippings
Salt and ground black pepper to taste

1. Reheat the pan you cooked your sausages in, which still has flecks of grease and burnt pork on the bottom.
2. When it's medium warm, pour in the beaten eggs and whisk as they cook.
3. Season with salt and pepper.

Serves 4

Notes on the Ever-popular, Ever-exalted Biscuit

If you're not a Cracker, you might be curious that this posterchild of Southern cuisine isn't on my list of top Cracker favorites, and for a simple reason: wheat really wasn't indigenous to the diet of the original *Crackus Americanis*. It was the food of the rich, the shining Buick of the quick-bread family; while cornbread was like a good farm truck: versatile and dependable, but a little déclassé.

Two examples of biscuit supremacy immediately leap to mind. The first is from my dear uncle Dennis whose family lost their two-mule farm outside of Cypress (Florida) in the Depression and were forced to move to a poorer farm. ("Land so poor you couldn't raise a *fuss* on it," he later complained.) He was just a small boy and hated the move. To soften the blow, his devoted mother would shape his cornbread into little biscuitlike rolls, so he wouldn't feel that they'd lost their place in society forever.

On my father's side of the family, so high did passions rise in the great biscuit/cornbread debate that it has forever scarred his enormous South Alabama clan. The details of the feud were related to me by my magnificent aunt Buenie. She recently told me that it all started back when her husband, Uncle Grover (a retired policeman from Phenix City, Alabama, of whom many stories are told) was a child working on Great-Uncle Len's farm. Apparently, Uncle Len ate hot biscuits for breakfast every morning but fed the boys (his nephew-cum-farmhands) cornbread.

" 'We ate cornbread, while he ate biscuit,' " Aunt Buenie quoted Uncle Grover. "*God,* he hated him for that."

Incidentally, Uncle Len and his brothers were also supposed to have "done away" with their stepfather (who was bad to drink and sent his children to work in the fields while he laid up drunk) and to have run off my own philandering grandfather (to Texas) under the threat of death. Apparently all of that was forgivable. What stuck in Uncle Grover's craw was the inequitable distribution of the family biscuits.

Roy's Famous Biscuits

I told Daddy I needed this recipe, and after much thought and consideration, he wrote out the directions for his famous biscuits, which I am inserting without editing so you can get the real Cracker Nuance. He walks you through this thing carefully, so pay attention, as he is serious about his biscuits and gives the directions in an unending SHOUT.

ROY'S FAMOUS BISCUIT RECIPE

YOU WILL NEED.

A HOT OVEN HEATED TO 425°–450° DEPENDING ON YOUR STOVE.

A GREASED IRON SKILLET—A 9" ONE WILL BE FINE.

A LARGE BOWL—PLASTIC WILL DO.

FOUR CUPS OF SELF RISING FLOUR—SIFTED IF NECESSARY.

½ CUP OF PURE LARD—IF HARD, CRUMBLE UP FINE AS YOU CAN.

BUTTERMILK AS NEEDED—DON'T OVER DO IT.

YOU WILL HAVE TO:

PUT 4 CUPS OF FLOUR IN BOWL.

PUT THE LARD IN BOWL AND MIX WITH THE FLOUR.

NOW COMES THE BEST PART.

WITH ONE HAND SLOWLY POUR IN THE BUTTERMILK.

START IN THE CENTER, WITH THE OTHER HAND

BLEND THE FLOUR IN A LITTLE AT THE TIME.

MIX THE DOUGH THE LARD AND THE MILK GOOD.

YOU DON'T WANT TO LEAVE ANY LUMPS IN THE MIX.

GO SLOW WITH THE MILK, YOU DON'T WANT THE DOUGH DRY,

BUT YOU DON'T WANT IT SOGGY AND STICKY EITHER.

I LIKE MINE SOFT BUT DRY.

ON A CUTTING BOARD OR CLEAN COUNTER TOP,

SPRINKLE SOME FLOUR AND PLACE THE DOUGH ON IT.

DON'T HANDLE THE DOUGH NO MORE THAN YOU HAVE TO.

WITH BOTH HANDS PRESS THE DOUGH TO ABOUT 1".

USING A CUTTER OR A GLASS, CUT OUT BISCUITS

PLACE IN FRYING SKILLET—I USE A FLAT ONE.

WITH A TABLE SPOON PLACE A LITTLE VEGETABLE OIL ON TOP OF
THE BISCUITS

PLACE IN OVEN FOR 10 MIN. MAY TAKE 15 MIN.

I LIKE MINE BROWN TOP AND BOTTOM

I PLACE THEM UNDER THE BROILER FOR ½ MIN. EACH.

ROY JOHNSON

OCALA FLA

I think Daddy's recipe is a good example of what comes when you cross-pollinate extreme fundamentalism and white flour: many directions and exhortations, and in the end, a promise of Heaven.

Need I say more?

Incidentally, on his draft, he included his address; go figure. Guess he thought I'd infringe his copyright or something and was making sure credit is given where credit is due. He's a ham radio fanatic, and if you are, too, give him a holler. His call sign is N4ZUA, and he's never met a ham he didn't like.

Notes on Quicker Biscuits

For all you lazy Crackers, here's a way to solve that age-old dilemma: I want a biscuit, but I don't want to cook. What you do is go to your local grocery store and find some precut frozen biscuits, not the pop-up kind but the ones in plastic freezer bags in the frozen-bread aisle. They are ready to toss on a greased baker and cook according to directions—no fuss, no complaint.

While they're baking, stir up a batch of gravy of your choice and sit down at the table with a cloth napkin and cup of hot coffee. Eat and be glad.

Tomato Gravy

Tomato Gravy is my hands-down favorite gravy on earth and around our house is eaten on hot biscuits. It isn't as popular as cream-based sawmill gravy, but it's beloved along the rim of the Gulf Coast, especially in west Florida and Louisiana, because a thousand tomatoes grow per bush and you can preserve every one of them, which gives you year-round tomatoes. We always ate this at breakfast, but I've heard of North Alabama Crackers eating it on roast and seafood, which seems a little sacrilegious to me, but to each his own. But do try it for breakfast on biscuits. You can't really call yourself a Cracker until you do.

2 tablespoons bacon or sausage drippings
2 tablespoons plain flour
One 16-ounce can stewed tomatoes, undrained
1 teaspoon salt
½ teaspoon ground black pepper
1¾ cups whole milk

1. Put the bacon drippings in a cast-iron skillet and heat over medium-high heat for 2 minutes.
2. Sprinkle the flour on the hot fat and turn the heat down to medium. Cook for about 1 minute, till the roux is light brown, stirring to make sure it doesn't burn.
3. Pour in the stewed tomatoes with the juice from the can. They will steam and crackle and send up a most pleasing cloud of gravy vapor.
4. Stir in the salt, pepper, and milk and cook over medium-low heat for 5 minutes.
5. Eat on top of split biscuits.

Makes 2 cups

Chocolate Gravy

My husband's maternal grandmother, Effie Neeley Hart, was a woman of formidable presence, famous for her chocolate gravy, which seasoned cooks will recognize as a close cousin to hot fudge sauce (a very close cousin). I met her when I was nineteen, on the eve of my wedding, when she came to Florida to vet her grandson's bride-to-be.

We were due to marry within the month and, as was the custom in those days, all our wedding presents were laid out in the living room so visitors could see what a popular couple we were. My own Grannie was eighty-one at the time and in poor health, living in a nursing home in Marianna, where she'd taken up oil painting. She'd been poor all her life and was beyond poor then. For my wedding present, instead of the usual towels or deviled egg plate, she had painted me a shaky-handed little oil painting of a mountain and a glade and had an aunt fix it up in a plastic gold frame.

I was proud of anything Grannie gave me, as I was of this, but was a little hesitant to show it to Wendel's fire-eating grandmother, who'd carried the conversation at the supper table with a skill that designated her, then and forever, as alpha female. She was poor as a church mouse herself but a great proponent of "bettering yourself." She had been impressed by Mama's china and further impressed by Daddy's twenty-minute supper prayer. I'd just gotten Grannie's present the day before and was massively protective of her. Privately I was a little afraid that Grannie Hart might look down her nose at it—think it cheap or poorly made. After supper, as I went down the present table, showing her our great cache of Tupperware and sheet sets, blenders, and flatware, I might have skipped over Grannie's painting altogether, if not for Mama, who was formidably alpha herself and never one to hide her light under a bushel.

She proudly lifted the painting from the table, held it up for Grannie Hart's inspection, and told her it was from my Grannie Rice—she'd painted it herself. She was an *artist,* see? She'd signed it and everything.

I was even hotter in the face after Mama's proud little exhibition, as we weren't talking about a Rembrandt here, but the product of a community education class at a Jackson County nursing home.

There was a pregnant pause while Grannie Hart held the little painting to the light and examined it through her bifocals. Then, with the magnificent generosity of women born poor, who knew the indignity of not having a dime to their names, she made a small show of turning and meeting our eye and declaiming with deadly earnestness, "Why, it's *beautiful*." Then, perhaps thinking her admiration hadn't hit a high-enough mark, she added without a hint of sarcasm, but just that great overflowing admiration, "Good as anything you could buy down at the Wal-Mart."

If I hadn't been in love with her grandson already, I would have fallen in love with him then.

Here is an early picture of her and her family, taken in central Arkansas, circa 1918. She is the pretty little blonde sitting on her mother's lap, with her poppa Sam and three of her sisters.

Behind them is the tent they lived in, as many Crackers did in the early years of the century. Grannie Hart died back in '04 and I write her name with honor: Effie Perilla Neeley Hart.

Here is her signature gravy, which she fixed my husband every morning of his life when he was a little boy, when his mother would drop him off at her house before school.

I bless her for that, too.

1 cup sugar

2 tablespoons plain flour

3 heaping tablespoons unsweetened
    cocoa powder

1½ cups whole milk

2 tablespoons sweet butter

1. Mix the sugar, flour, and cocoa in a heavy-bottomed saucepan until well blended. Stir in the milk.

2. Cook, stirring constantly, over medium heat till thickened like gravy. Add the butter and stir till smooth.

Makes 2½ cups

Melon Slices

Melons were once a summertime pleasure, but these days they're available just about year-round. They are the perfect addition to any breakfast, a cool light dessert that will brighten the most overcast dawn.

1 cantaloupe
2 honeydew melons
½ teaspoon salt

Halve the melons, remove the seeds, and cut off the rinds. Thinly slice the fruit and lay out on a platter. Lightly sprinkle with salt.

Serves 6

V. POKER NIGHT

Poker nights are a well-loved tradition in Crackerland, where card games in all their infinite variety thrive, despite the best efforts of the good women of my grandmother's day, who thought playing cards the invention of Satan. There was, in fact, the threat of a game gone bad, where an otherwise conscientious father might put his family in financial jeopardy, hence, I expect, the fear the game inspired. These days that threat is minimized by house rules that preclude anyone losing the deed to his land or otherwise incurring his wife's eternal wrath. These less-threatening games are generally played among old and chummy buddies who meet at appointed times—Monday nights or first Fridays—or they're more randomly spaced and open to guests.

In Wendel's group, the food is as much a draw as the fall of the cards, and there is a certain competition over who makes the best chili, appetizer, or dessert. They are as vain as any woman about their cooking skills and especially fond of creating some sort of big-hit signature dish, preferably one with really hot peppers. Since we're talking men here, whatever you make, make a lot of it.

Poker Night Chili

Chili is great for men-parties—Superbowl Sundays or poker nights—because it is bountiful and masculine and fairly easy to make. Since the abundance of beans will almost inevitably result in the passing of gas, it also has a certain entertainment value later in the evening, especially if the cards aren't falling your way.

1 pound lean ground beef
1 cup chopped yellow onion
½ teaspoon red pepper flakes
3 tablespoons chili powder
2 teaspoons minced garlic
¼ teaspoon curry powder
1 bay leaf
One 14-ounce can diced tomatoes
One 15-ounce can kidney beans, drained
One 16-ounce can tomato sauce
1 cup commercial salsa

1. Cook the ground beef, onion, and red pepper flakes in a large saucepan or stockpot until the beef is browned. Drain off the excess fat.

2. Add the remaining ingredients, bring to a low boil, then simmer uncovered over medium-low heat for at least 1 hour.

Serves 6

Cheesy French Bread

This bread is sinfully cheesy and perfect with chili.

1 large loaf French bread
1 cup shredded Swiss cheese
1 cup shredded Cheddar cheese
½ cup mayonnaise
1 envelope Italian salad dressing mix
½ cup diced yellow onion

1. Preheat the oven to 350°.

2. Split the loaf of bread lengthwise in half.

3. Mix the cheeses, mayonnaise, and salad dressing seasoning in a medium bowl.

4. Lay the bread on a cookie sheet. Mound the cheese mixture in the middle of the split bread and sprinkle with the onion.

5. Bake for 8 to 10 minutes, till the cheese is bubbly.

6. Cut into 1-inch-thick slices.

Serves 6 to 8

Salmon Patties with Dill Sauce

Salmon patties are the Cracker's answer to crab cakes. I grew up eating them and to this day, pronounce the "l"—which I understand is a sure sign of a country upbringing. For a time, I tried to remember to say *sa-mon,* but it never came easy. I had that uncomfortable pause before speaking, as in, "Hey, d'you want a (pause, look of serious concentration) sa—mon patty?"

That pause speaks of insecurity with living in the mainstream.

That pause is all Cracker.

This little Cracker dish (which does indeed include crackers, lowercase) comes with a delicious dill sauce, and those are two Ls you can pronounce boldly, without fear of public censure.

One 16-ounce can salmon, drained
1 small yellow onion, finely chopped
Freshly ground black pepper, to taste
2 large eggs, well beaten
1 to 1½ cups crushed butter crackers
3 tablespoons sweet butter

1. Put the salmon in a medium bowl. Add the onion and pepper, then the eggs, mixing well.

2. Mix in the cracker crumbs and shape into little patties, about 2 inches wide and ½ inch thick.

3. Melt the butter in a cast-iron skillet over medium heat. Add as many patties as will fit and fry for about 1 minute on each side, till golden brown.

Makes about 1 dozen

DILL SAUCE

    1 cup sour cream

    ½ cup mayonnaise

    2 teaspoons dried or chopped fresh dill

    2 tablespoons fresh lemon juice

    1 teaspoon salt

    ½ teaspoon sugar

Put all the ingredients in a small bowl and mix till smooth. Serve alongside the salmon patties.

Makes 1¾ cups

Little Smokies in Grape Jelly

Yes, you heard that right, Little Smokies (the ever-popular cocktail wiener) cooked in grape jelly. This proves once and for all that where pork and sugar are concerned, there is just no way to go wrong. It's an especially good recipe for the hard-working, poker-playing bachelor, who can cook his wienies at home in the Crock-Pot while he earns his paycheck. It's called Cracker multitasking.

2 packages Little Smokies
One 12-ounce bottle chili sauce
1 cup grape jelly

Combine the cocktail wieners, chili sauce, and grape jelly in a slow cooker. Cover and cook on low for 6 to 8 hours.

Serves 5

Pork Stackers

This recipe requires a little forethought and a day's preparation, but the steps are simple and the slow cooker does most of the work. You can make it in advance and freeze it, then later microwave it and put the topping on before serving.

> **One 4-pound Boston butt**
> **One 16-ounce package dried pinto beans**
> **2 cloves garlic, minced**
> **1 cup chopped Vidalia onion**
> **1 tablespoon salt**
> **1 teaspoon red pepper flakes**
> **One 13-ounce bag white corn tortilla chips**
> **1 cup each shredded Cheddar cheese, sour cream,**
>   **shredded lettuce, and chopped tomatoes**
> **Salsa and hot sauce for serving**

1. The day before serving, put the pork roast, pinto beans, garlic, onion, and seasonings in a large slow cooker and add water to cover.

2. Cover and cook on low all day, till the pork has fallen to pieces and the beans have become the consistency of bean dip. Add more water if necessary.

3. Line a large baking dish (or two if necessary) with a layer of tortilla chips, then spoon the pork mixture on top.

4. On top of that, layer shredded cheese, sour cream, shredded lettuce, chopped tomatoes, and whatever other ingredient strikes your fancy.

5. Serve with salsa and hot sauce.

Serves 8 to 10

Hot Peppered Pecans

No gathering of Cracker men is complete without a dish hot enough to test their mettle and turn at least part of the evening into a who-can-eat-the-hottest-pepper contest. These peppered pecans aren't really lethal. They can be made hotter by adding a little habanero pepper sauce or less hot by using plain old hot sauce.

3 tablespoons butter
1 to 1½ teaspoons hot sauce
1 clove garlic, minced
½ teaspoon salt
3 cups pecan halves

1. Preheat the oven to 350°.

2. Melt the butter in a small skillet. Stir in the hot sauce, garlic, and salt and sauté for a minute or so. Add the pecans and toss to coat them with the sauce.

3. Spread the pecans in a single layer on a cookie sheet and bake for 1 hour, giving the pan a shake a few times to make sure they're cooking evenly.

Makes 3 cups

CHAPTER FIVE

Pickles, Preserves, and Things in Jars

L ike most Crackers of his generation, Granddaddy prided himself on being self-sufficient. On his narrow, four-acre farm on the west end of Marianna, he produced everything from prize-winning sows to a thriving truck garden. He not only fed his family off the produce but also went around Marianna on a mule-drawn wagon, selling fresh corn and tomatoes, sweet potatoes, peppers, and cucumbers to the city folk downtown. For cash, he distilled pine resin into turpentine, which he sold door to door, and grew his own fruit: scuppernongs, figs, plums, and high-quality Curtis pecans, which he sold to the candy company in December for Christmas money.

Thanks to his industry, Grannie was able to pickle and can and "put up" all manner of fruit and produce, nearly year-round. Like all good Cracker wives, she prided herself on the contents of her pie safe in the kitchen. From summer to summer, year round, there were shelves and shelves of jars filled with pickles, peppers, jams, and jellies, glimmering with the jewel tones of the past year's crop. They were a great source of pride and were handed out to friends and family, with the jar's contents printed on little labels on the front, along with the year they were made. Like quilt making or crocheting, stocking a pie safe was a Cracker work of art, one much easier to duplicate these days with modern stoves and packaged pectin. The flavor is so much better than store-bought jellies and jams. It will give you, as the used car salesmen used to say, "the pride of ownership."

Pepper Sauce

I'm beginning with a true basic of Cracker cooking that applies to almost every meal in this book—pepper sauce. Crackers put this sauce on everything: pork chops, greens, you name it. The peppers are usually little hot peppers, the kind you grow in a corner of your backyard. In the past few years, a cult of pepper love has taken hold, and people have begun using datil (hotter) or jalapeño peppers, or, if you really equate hot with virility, habaneros, which are (in my humble opinion) just about too hot to eat. Daddy prides himself on his ability to eat fire, but even he makes do with the lowly little Tabasco pepper, which is as prolific as an okra bush.

Peppers of any variety
White vinegar

Peppers are easily preserved because they're so dang hot. Daddy and Wendel just stick them in a bottle or any other container, really. (Daddy puts fiery habaneros in an old Country Time Lemonade jar.) Cover them with vinegar and there you go. As you consume your peppers, you'll have to add more, and as you run out of vinegar, you'll have to add more of that. The more vinegar you add, the milder the pepper sauce becomes. If you're starting out with datils or habaneros, that's probably a *good* thing.

Pickled Okra

Pickled Okra is a good addition to any relish tray or dinner table. You can make them as hot as you want. These are only mildly spicy. Slip a jalapeño or datil pepper into every jar, and you'll have a considerably hotter product.

7 cloves garlic, peeled
1 tablespoon red pepper flakes
4 pounds young okra pods, washed
    and trimmed
7 teaspoons chopped fresh dill
1 quart white vinegar
1 cup water
½ cup pickling salt

1. Place 1 clove garlic and a sprinkle of red pepper flakes into each of 7 hot sterilized pint jars.
2. Pack the jars firmly with okra, then add 1 teaspoon chopped dill to each.
3. Combine the vinegar, water, and salt in a large saucepan and bring to a boil.
4. Pour over the okra, then screw the metal bands on tightly.
5. Process for 10 minutes in a boiling water bath.
6. Let the pickles stand for a month before opening.

Makes 7 pints

Fig Preserves

Most Cracker homesteads had a clump of fig trees, and since they bear on and off for a good part of the year, figs were a popular item at the breakfast table. Granddaddy's fig trees were the size of dogwood trees, but Uncle Kelly didn't like figs, so Grannie would add some strawberry jelly powder to the mixture and pretend it was strawberry preserves. Apparently Uncle Kelly bought it.

These are particularly good on pancakes with butter. If you're into making crepes, insert a dollop of fig preserves and sweetened sour cream. The sour cream cuts some of the fig sugar, and what you will have is a fine example of French-Cracker fusion. Sublime.

5 pounds fresh figs, trimmed and washed
5 pounds sugar
Several thin lemon slices to keep it from turning
    (if you like natural-colored figs)

1. Put the figs in a large pot, cover with sugar, and let sit overnight.

2. In the morning, cook the mixture over medium heat till the sugar is dissolved. Turn down the heat and simmer quietly for a couple of hours. They're done when cooked to the consistency of table syrup with a few figs still identifiable as figs, more or less.

3. Remove from the heat and put up in sterilized jars. Insert a few lemon slices if you want them to retain a more greenish color. (Grannie never did and I like my figs as brown as chocolate. But that's just me.) Process in boiling water, then seal according to manufacturer's directions.

Makes 5 pints

Orange Marmalade

Some people like blueberries in the morning, but I like the zest of citrus. Since this isn't a jelly, it's more or less foolproof and good on both toast and biscuits.

6 oranges, peeled
1 lemon, unpeeled
11 cups cold water
7 cups sugar

1. With a sharp knife, remove all the white membrane from the peeled oranges and slice thin. Thinly slice the unpeeled lemon.

2. Put the oranges and lemon in a large bowl, cover with the water, and chill overnight.

3. Put the orange mixture in a large heavy-bottomed saucepan. Simmer uncovered for 3 hours. Add the sugar, turn up the heat, and bring to a low boil. Slowly boil for 1 hour, till thick; stir often to make sure it doesn't scorch.

4. Process in boiling water, then pour into sterilized jars and seal.

Makes 5 pints

Refrigerator Strawberry Jam

This is a tried-and-true method of making nearly sureproof strawberry jam, with none of the worry of the jelly not jelling. This jelly will jell.

2 cups mashed fresh strawberries
4 cups sugar
One 1.75-ounce box fruit pectin
¾ cup water

1. Mix the strawberries and sugar and set aside.
2. Stir the pectin and water in a saucepan. Bring to a boil, stirring constantly, and boil for 1 minute. Remove from the heat.
3. Add the strawberries to the pectin and stir till the sugar is completely dissolved and the mixture is no longer grainy.
4. Pour into plastic freezer containers and let cool completely. Store in the freezer till ready to use. Store in the refrigerator after opening.

Makes four 8-ounce containers

Mayhaw Jelly

Mayhaw trees grow wild in swamps all over the South. Native Crackers are fond of making jelly from the berries, but let me warn you beforehand: We're making real jelly here, which can be as temperamental as divinity. Unlike most Cracker recipes, this one requires close measurement, or your jelly won't jell, and you'll have a few quarts of very sweet mayhaw nectar on your hands.

8 cups mayhaw berries, stemmed and cleaned
One 1.35-ounce box fruit pectin
7 cups sugar

1. Crush and force the mayhaw through a sieve till you have 5 cups of juice.
2. Pour the mayhaw juice into a large pot and heat over medium heat for 1 minute. Add the pectin and stir till dissolved.
3. Add the sugar and bring to a boil over high heat. Boil for 1 minute, then remove from the heat.
4. Skim off the foam and ladle the liquid into hot jars, leaving ½-inch headspace.
5. Cover the jars with hot lids and screw the bands on firmly.
6. Process for 5 minutes in a boiling water bath. Remove and let cool.

Makes about 11 half-pints

Scuppernong Jelly

One way to locate an original Cracker homestead is to search for the presence of either a coral vine or a scuppernong vine growing wild in the woods. Crackers loved both of them because they were easy to grow and made for a bit of welcome shade. The scuppernongs were grown on giant arbors spacious enough to sit under, so there's many a Cracker who got engaged under the shade of a scuppernong arbor.

The thick-skinned little grape could be eaten fresh or made into a number of familiar Cracker dishes: jelly for the pie safe, or even scuppernong wine. My aunt made scuppernong wine but regrettably didn't pass down the recipe. We'll have to make do with the jelly, which is clearer and lighter than grape jelly, and transforms the most timid biscuit into a masterpiece.

4 cups scuppernong juice
2 teaspoons fresh lemon juice
One 1.35-ounce box fruit pectin
7 cups sugar

1. Crush and force the scuppernong through a sieve till you have 4 cups of juice.
2. Bring the scuppernong juice, lemon juice, and pectin to a boil in a large heavy-bottomed pot. Add the sugar and stir well.
3. Boil for a minute or two, then remove from the heat.
4. Pour the jelly into hot sterilized jars, leaving ½-inch headspace. Cover the jars with hot lids and screw the bands on firmly.
5. Process for 5 minutes in a boiling water bath. Remove and let cool.

Makes 8 half-pints

Pickled Eggs

This strange little treat is often sold at the counter of corner stores in big jars, next to big jars of pickled pig feet. They are good travelers and a nice tart side dish to complement a bland meat.

2 cups white vinegar
1 cup water
1 tablespoon salt
1 teaspoon ground black pepper
1 teaspoon dry mustard
2 dozen eggs, hard-boiled and shelled
3 hot chile peppers
1 medium yellow onion, cut into rings

1. Heat the vinegar, water, salt, pepper, and dry mustard to boiling in a medium saucepan.
2. Divide the peeled eggs, chile peppers, and onion rings among three 1-quart jars.
3. Pour the vinegar mixture over the eggs and seal the jars.
4. Let stand for 1 week before eating.

Makes 3 quarts

Fresh Garlic Dill Pickles

If you don't have room for a huge store of pickle jars, this recipe will give you wonderfully garlicky pickles, six quarts at a time. The secret is fresh dill, which is sold in the produce section of your grocery store.

3 to 4 pounds small pickling cucumbers
8 cloves garlic, peeled and slightly crushed
1 dozen or so long sprigs fresh dill
4 quarts water
4 cups white vinegar
¾ teaspoon salt

1. Wash the cucumbers, then pack them, standing upright, in sterilized 1-quart jars.
2. Put a crushed garlic clove and a few sprigs of dill in each jar.
3. Bring the water, vinegar, and salt to a boil in a large pan. Pour the brine over the pickles.
4. Cover the jars with hot lids and screw the bands on firmly.
5. Process in a boiling water bath for 5 to 10 minutes.
6. Let stand for 1 week before eating.

Makes 6 or 7 quarts

CHAPTER SIX

The Cracker Pantry

Here are a few handy things to have around the house in pursuit of the Cracker dream. Cast-iron frying pans are handed down in Cracker country, all seasoned and black and ready to fry up a plate of chicken. If you buy one new, read the manufacturer's instructions on how to season it (basically grease and bake till black). It takes a few hours and makes your house smell like burnt iron for a while, but the resulting pan will be practically indestructible.

Cast-iron frying pan with lid
Cast-iron Dutch oven with lid
2-quart pot with lid
Heavy-bottomed medium saucepan
Baking sheet
9 x 13-inch baking pan
Tube cake pan
12-count muffin pan
Butcher knife

Serrated knife
Tongs for frying
Heavy wooden spoon
Half-gallon pitcher

DRY PANTRY

Self-rising cornmeal
Plain cornmeal
Granulated sugar
Powdered sugar
Brown sugar
Light corn syrup
Dark corn syrup
Plain flour
Self-rising flour
Baking soda
Baking powder
Grits
Hot sauce
Peanut oil
Lard
Pecans
Dried minced onion
Red pepper flakes
Dried dill (though fresh is better)
Dried rosemary
Garlic powder
Regular salt
Grinder of sea salt
Seasoning salt
Onion salt
Pepper mill filled with black peppercorns
Real vanilla extract (not flavoring)
Brandy flavoring
Soy sauce

Mayonnaise
White vinegar

I wouldn't stock up on perishable refrigerated items, but I am listing them so you'll take notice when you walk through the grocery store, as they will eventually appear in a recipe list.

Butter
Cheddar cheese
Sour cream
Buttermilk
Cream cheese
Eggs
Whipped topping

And last, but certainly not least, are a few recipes that are repeat performers at just about any Cracker feast.

Iced Tea

I have two recipes for that serene nectar of the gods, iced tea. What more can I say about this all-powerful liquid? It has caffeine. It has sugar. It has good antioxidants and will make your soul sing. It is the single item in the Cracker repertoire I couldn't live without, though old-timers were equally fond of ice water. In their day, it was a delicacy, and old Cracker daddies had an annoying habit of making their wives and children fetch it for them whenever they wanted it. I have never been a great fetcher for anyone, and tea is my own obsession.

I am giving you the straight scoop on how I make it, though mileage varies, as do recipes. Burger makes hers with one brand and swears by it, and I use another, the same one Aunt Doris told me to use thirty years ago. Some people put in lemon or mint, but I leave mine cold and strong and a little less sweet than the liquid sugar you get in restaurants. It's simple to make. Anyone who tells you otherwise is trying to blind you with science.

The truth is tea can be as sweet as you can stand it or made with no sugar at all. You can drink it either cold and straight, or over ice for a slightly diluted product. I drink mine cold and straight, but that's just me. If I have to have ice, I prefer crushed ice, so I can crack my teeth eating the leftovers. Just buy some tea bags and white sugar and experiment. In no time at all you'll be pontificating about your own iced-tea preferences, proving once and for all that you are a Cracker who knows his (or her) way around the kitchen.

2 quarts water, divided
4 family-sized tea bags
1 cup or so sugar

1. Fill a large kettle or medium saucepan with 1 quart fresh water. Heat over high heat for about 4 minutes.

2. Just before it boils (little bubbles will appear on the sides), move it off the burner and toss in the tea bags.

3. Put something on top to trap the steam (Mama used to put a china saucer on the top of her kettle) and let steep for at least 10 minutes.

4. Pour the sugar into a half-gallon pitcher and add the still-warm tea. Stir, then add the remaining 1 quart water and stir a little more.

5. You can serve it over ice now, but I prefer to put a lid on the pitcher and chill it in the refrigerator till it gets nice and cold, so I don't have to dilute it with too much ice.

Makes 2 quarts

Light Lemony Iced Tea

I first had this fusion iced tea at the reception for my daughter's wedding in St. Augustine. And though I am a purist where tea is concerned and usually detest strange fruity iced teas (especially raspberry, which puts me in a foul temper whenever I eat somewhere that serves it exclusively), I found this mix of tea and lemonade and crushed mint strangely addictive. The fresh mint gives it a slight tang. Since I've poured on the sugar in the dessert section (and the pork section, *and* the salad section), I'm offering this version sugar-free, made with artificially sweetened lemonade. That way, you can drink a whole pitcher without guilt, as you eat a piece of pound cake.

2 family-sized tea bags
2 quarts water, at room temperature
½ cup sugar-free lemonade mix powder
3 or 4 fresh mint leaves, crushed
½ lemon, sliced

1. Steep the tea bags in 1 quart of the water in a half-gallon pitcher for 10 minutes. Add the lemonade mix and stir.

2. Fill the pitcher to the top with crushed ice and water and stir well.

3. Add the mint leaves and lemon slices and stir some more. Remove the tea bags and drink in joy, without fear of excess.

Makes 2 quarts

Perfect Coffee

When I was a young wife, my dear aunt Doris gave me the secret to her never-fail coffee, which I have reduced to a formula. She made it this way every day of her married life and had a very long and happy marriage. I think there is a connection there somewhere. Here is the formula: Folger's coffee + water + stainless-steel percolator + a little canned milk = a great cup of coffee.

I am often seduced into buying fancy grind-and-brew systems and don't always make it this way, but whenever I do, it is perfection in a cup.

Katie B's Rolls

Here is my single recipe for rising bread, or white bread as it is known in Crackerdom, where cornbread reigns supreme. Rolls are reserved for Sunday when they can be made in advance and popped into the oven as soon as you get home from church, then eaten hot. This is the only way to serve white bread to a Cracker, as serving packaged sliced white bread at any sit-down meal is an affront to the culture and punishable by excommunication. My husband is from Arkansas, and he sometimes does it because Arkansans must eat either rice or bread with every meal or they will die. This is not a tradition south of the black belt. If my sainted mother ever saw such a thing on her table, she'd fall over in a dead faint. To her, sliced white bread has its place in bologna sandwiches and toast with jelly, but little else. It certainly has no place of value on the table, where it would indicate a severe lack of social refinement. The people who eat sliced white bread at a sit-down meal also drink instant tea and imported beer and will insist on arguing politics. Let their dining companions beware.

My recipe (or rather, Katie B's recipe) yields a much more palatable white bread—one that can be made into cinnamon rolls with the addition of butter and cinnamon, or shaped into cloverleaf rolls or little twists. When my girls were small, Katie B used to invite them over to teach them how to make her dough. She made it once a week and would warm the leftovers for use all week long. I thought it was an old pioneer recipe passed along like sourdough starter, but when I asked, she said she'd lifted the original recipe from the back of a Fleischmann's yeast package in the early thirties and had never had reason to look for another. Over the years she'd made a few adjustments, but Mr. Fleischmann was her original inspiration.

2 packages active dry yeast

¼ cup warm water, lukewarm to the touch

2 cups whole milk

2 large eggs, separated

2 tablespoons sugar

1 teaspoon salt

6 cups plain flour (half whole wheat, half white)

Handful of wheat germ (so Katie B once instructed me)

5 tablespoons melted salted butter, plus more for brushing

1. Sprinkle the yeast over the warm water in a large bowl, let stand 5 minutes, and stir until dissolved.

2. Add the milk, egg yolks, sugar, and salt and mix thoroughly. Stir in the flour until a sticky dough forms.

3. Beat the egg whites in a small bowl until combined, then stir into the flour mixture. Stir in the melted butter. If your dough is too wet to handle, you can add a little more flour (not too much, or you'll have dry rolls). Toss in a handful of wheat germ.

4. This isn't a wrestling-match bread recipe where you have to pound the dough into submission. Just leisurely knead till the dough is smooth and elastic. Place the dough in a greased large bowl and cover with a kitchen towel. Let rise in a warm place for about 1 hour.

5. Punch down the dough and roll into whatever shape you like: twists, cloverleaves, old-fashioned cut-out rising biscuits, you choose.

6. Put the rolls on a greased baking sheet and brush with a little more melted butter. Let rise covered for another hour or so.

7. Preheat the oven to 375°.

8. Bake the rolls for 15 minutes or so, till brown on the top, depending on how big they are.

9. Brush the baked rolls with additional melted butter, and if you want a more sophisticated little roll, sprinkle it with dried dill, sesame seeds, or even dried onion flakes.

*Makes 1 to 2 dozen,
depending on how you shape them*

Flaky Pie Crust

Since I haven't been shy about the use of fat till now, I'm going whole hog and giving you the old-school recipe for pie crust, made with lard. If you really can't bring yourself to cook with lard, substitute cold vegetable shortening. But lard will make it ultra flaky, and since it isn't used very much these days, will leave your guests thinking, "How *does* she do it?"

You can keep the secret ingredient to yourself. When their favorite blue jeans no longer zip, they'll be none the wiser.

2⅔ cups plain flour
¾ teaspoon salt
8 ounces lard, chilled
⅓ to ½ cup cold water

1. Blend the flour and salt in a large bowl.

2. With a fork or two knives (or better yet, a pastry blender), cut the lard into the flour till it is about as coarse as cornmeal.

3. Gradually mix in enough of the cold water for the dough to stick together. Divide in half and flatten into two rounds.

4. Since you make these two at a time, freeze one and chill the other. After the dough has sat in the refrigerator for at least 30 minutes, take it out and roll with a rolling pin into a circle on a floured surface.

5. Carefully transfer it to a 9-inch pie plate. Trim the edge, and if it tears or acts ornery, just patch it up the best you can. This isn't a beauty contest; it's a lard-based pie crust. Trust me when I say it will be eaten, flawless or not.

6. Wrap the extra pie crust and freeze till use.

Makes two 9-inch pie crusts

Graham Cracker Crust

This is an all-purpose graham cracker crust that can be used with all cream pies. If you're adventuresome, you can add a pinch of cinnamon or ¼ cup ground nuts.

2 cups graham cracker crumbs
¼ cup sugar
¼ cup sweet butter, melted

1. Preheat the oven to 350°.

2. Mix the graham cracker crumbs and sugar together in a mixing bowl. Add the butter and stir well.

3. Pour the mixture into a 9-inch pie plate and press evenly over the bottom and up the sides.

4. Bake for 6 to 7 minutes to set.

Makes one 9-inch pie crust

CHAPTER SEVEN

Thoughts in Closing

Since Crackers equate food with the sacred, I feel inclined to tie up our nostalgic journey into the soul of Cracker essence with a few thoughts on that essential part of any Cracker meal, no matter how proud or how humble: the Blessing. It is variously referred to as Giving Thanks or Saying Grace, but all it really boils down to is a simple statement of gratitude to God, or Jesus, or a Higher Power, or Heavenly Parent, or whomever you regularly pray to. You can insert your own Higher Power (and, baby, you know I got mine: number two on list above, Son of Number One).

In His Name we pray around here, but if you don't around your house, that is certainly your call. One of the reasons our old Cracker ancestors went to the great trouble of pulling up stakes in Wales and Scotland and all points east to come to our scrubby, mosquito-bitten shores was to practice the Freedom of Religion, and I'm all about that. But religion aside, I like the idea of Giving Thanks, of pausing on the edge of pleasure and being grateful for our wonderful American bounty, which is pretty dang impressive by any standard at all.

For the uninitiated or the shy, here's how it goes. If you're around a close table, then hold hands. If you're in a crowd, just bow your head and say Grace (or the Blessing; it all means the same thing). If you truly don't know a blessing, I submit two for your consideration. The first is usually for children; the second, muttered lightning quick by the hurried and the famished in a last-minute diversion before their long-winded grandpa lets go a two-minute prayer-sermon and the cornbread gets cold. Both are suitable for mixed-religious gatherings and are agreeable in both simplicity and form. If you're new to saying the blessing, no worries; they have a pleasing tempo and after a few tries you'll gain speed and confidence.

"God is great, God is good, let us thank Him for our food.
By His hands, we are fed; give us Lord our daily bread.
Ah-men."

Or, for our Lazy Cracker friends,

"Give us grateful hearts for these and all our blessings, Ah-men."

If neither really suits you, then call up your oldest living relative and ask how he or she used to bless their food. Adjust according to current beliefs. If on the odd chance you're a Cracker atheist, I don't know what to tell you. Hell, just *eat.* (And, yes, such a creature really does exist. My cousin David Blair's paternal great-grandfather was as Cracker a Cracker as ever lived, in the Oxford area of central Florida, and he was an atheist. Back then, he was called a Free Thinker. He was a prosperous farmer, and when his son got saved in the early twenties, the old man pitched a fit. He simply forbid him to walk the Christian walk, and such was his implacable will that his son renounced his conversion and went buck-wild. He was so wild, in fact, that his father called him in a year later and gave him permission to reconvert, telling him, "I'd rather have a Christian for a son than a reprobate.")

So, see? Diversity abounds. And incidentally, the son in question went on to become a great Pentecostal preacher and a hero of my childhood: Old Brother Blair. He baptized my mother and married my parents and preached many a family funeral. I am personally glad his father unbent and allowed him to exercise his right to religious freedom and return to the Lord. Since he's been dead half a dozen years, I'm sure he is, too.

• • •

Here's my favorite family dinner portrait, taken long before I was born, of Granddaddy, Grannie, Linda Ann, Aunt Doris, and Mama.

Aunt Doris, who was merrily skeptical of Grannie's hard-line religion, is obviously telling a joke on the tail end of the prayer, while Linda Ann and Grannie still have their eyes shut. Granddaddy, who (you might recall) was something of a skeptic himself, is the only one laughing. Mama's back is to the camera, so you can't see her response. I'd bet she was laughing, too. Aunt Doris was hard to resist and never funnier than when needling the status quo. In her hand is a cup of her magnificent coffee, yet another reason to smile.

So here we are at the end of our journey, or at least at the end of the beginning, as Cracker Cooking is a living entity and continues to mutate and adapt with admirable results. Whereas it was once a hard-to-explain offshoot of Low Country or Soul Food, it is now openly cooked and eaten in public with no apologies to anyone. I take this as a healthy sign of our emerging Cracker consciousness. We're neglected and occasionally shiftless and have less pigmentation than a boiled egg, but so what?

Let he who is without sin cast the first stone. We are who we are and that is a great way to be. To the doubters and the unsure, I say: Embrace your Crackerness, my friends. Cook gravy for breakfast and don't sweat the small stuff. Lounge on the porch. Loiter at the post office. If your e-mail crashes at work, exclaim, "I de*clare"* in a loud and pained voice. Don't hide your light under a bushel, or we might end up like the poor old Hoover Hogs, ten feet down a tunnel in a forgotten field, afraid to show our gopher faces. Be bold and be strong, and listen, if you're Jersey-born or Cuban or Vietnamese, don't think you're out of the loop. The essence of our Crackerness is our ability to adjust and absorb, to welcome and to embrace.

Our independence of thought may make us seem untenable and clannish, but in our old Cracker way, we are tolerant of other foods, thoughts, and cultures and always curious to know how they do it "out there." If we weren't, we wouldn't be here. As I said earlier, our base was Scotch-Irish, Native American of all stripes, Spanish conquistador, African, and a pinch of everything from Moravian immigrant to Jewish trader. Our end will be all of the above, with a dash of every other addition under the sun: Vietnamese, Cuban, Puerto Rican, Californian, and, yes, my friends, even a few old Yanks.

I urge my fellow Crackers (who fainted at that last one) to readjust old expectations and embrace diversity. If you can't do it out of love, then do it out of pity. Think of it this way: They didn't have the pleasure of being born here, but got here as quick as they could. Feed them enough tomato gravy, and they'll become more Cracker than Cracker. They will leap to a fight with anyone who hints otherwise.

If you worry such an open-handed invitation will somehow dilute the species, let not your heart be troubled. To paraphrase scripture: Greater is the cornbread within us than the white bread that is in the world.

And I don't mean that sacrilegiously. I mean it sincerely.

Eat and enjoy, amen.

Janis Owens
Newberry, Florida
Home of big-boned women and my own gopher-turtle village;
cooking supper as I speak.

ACKNOWLEDGMENTS

Many people have supported this project from the beginning, and great thanks go to Cracker expert Dana Ste. Claire, who told me I must write a Cracker cookbook and made me think I wouldn't get into heaven otherwise. Also, to Marly, Beth, and Whitney, and all the fierce women of New York, who grasped my vision and equaled my enthusiasm from day one. I offer my love and thanks to my tribe of handsome cousins: Michael, Marcie, Nelson; the Marianna folk and the illustrious Alabama Johnsons; plus my far-flung Georgia cousins, who donated pictures and stories and great love (Junior, Charlotte, Sandi, and Joyce, I'm talking to you); and the church family I grew up with, who helped turn me into the spoiled white woman I am today. And finally, for all the readers and fellow Crackers I've met on the road these past ten years, who lit up when I used the word, and my black friends and family (yes, Ava, I'm talking to you), who roared with laughter. Your enthusiasm and your stories helped me remember who I am—and that, my friends, is a great gift. Here's hoping we meet for supper soon.

INDEX

Printed in the United States
By Bookmasters